Wake Up and Change Your Life

ALSO BY DUNCAN BANNATYNE:

Anyone Can Do It: My Story

Wake Up
and Change Your Life

Duncan Bannatyne

This edition first published in Great Britain in 2008 by
Orion Books
an imprint of the Orion Publishing Group Ltd
Orion House, 5 Upper St Martin's Lane, London WC2H 9EA

An Hachette Livre UK Company

1 3 5 7 9 10 8 6 4 2

A CIP catalogue record for this book is available from the British Library.

ISBN: 978 0 7528 9141 5 (hardback)
ISBN: 978 0 7528 9142 2 (export trade paperback)

Printed in Great Britain by Clays Ltd, St Ives plc

The Orion Publishing Group's policy is to use papers that are natural, renewable and recyclable and made from wood grown in sustainable forests. The logging and manufacturing processes are expected to conform to the environmental regulations of the country of origin.

Every effort has been made to fulfil requirements with regard to reproducing copyright material. The author and publisher will be glad to rectify any omissions at the earliest opportunity.

www.orionbooks.co.uk

Contents

TO MY CHILDREN

Abigail, Hollie, Jennifer, Eve, Emily and Tom.

Remember I love you more…

Acknowledgements

First and foremost I would like to thank my beautiful wife, Joanne, and my children, Abigail, Hollie, Jennifer, Eve, Emily and Tom. Thank you and I love you all so much.

I would like to thank Jo Monroe for working with me a second time; it has been an absolute pleasure. Thanks also to Ian Marshall at the Orion Publishing Group and Jonny Geller at Curtis Brown; your help with this book has been invaluable.

Finally, I would like to thank the ten entrepreneurs who took time out from their busy lives to kindly write a case study: Alexander Amosu, Anthony Coates-Smith, Simon Woodroffe, OBE, Kanya King, MBE, Chris Gorman, OBE, James Caan, Eugenie Harvey, Grant Morgan, Damaris Evans and Ray Taylor.

A big thank you to everyone.

Introduction

At the age of 30, I was a penniless beach bum. At the age of 37, I was a millionaire. I honestly believe that anyone – absolutely anyone – can do exactly what I did and turn their life around; you just need to wake up to the possibilities that are all around you and make a decision to change your life.

I left school at 15 without any qualifications. At 19, I was dishonourably discharged from the Royal Navy. For the next ten years I made ends meet with a series of dead-end jobs – cabbying, selling ice creams on the beach, bar work, fixing up old motors – until I found myself sitting on a beach one day wondering where I was headed. I wanted to get married and start a family, and that meant I needed to find a way of earning more money than I could pick up with casual jobs. However, I wasn't qualified for anything and I was unemployable in any profession that paid well. I really didn't have many options. However, I had just read a piece in a newspaper about a guy who had started a business from scratch and had made his first million. His name was Alan Sugar. As I sat on that beach, I decided that this was my wake-up call. I was going to do exactly what this Alan Sugar had done: I was going to change my life and make myself a million.

Starting a business is, I believe, the best option for people whose skills don't fit the job marketplace. For all those people who don't fit into Human Resources recruitment pigeon holes – too young, too old, not enough experience, over-qualified, criminal record – working for yourself is the most enjoyable and lucrative option if you want a meaningful career. And for everyone who finds themselves in jobs where they spend most of their day watching the clock in return for a modest wage, then becoming an entrepreneur means an end to low pay, and low esteem. It might also make you very rich.

Perhaps you've invented something, maybe you've discovered a gap in the market, or possibly – like me when I was 30 – you don't know what business you want to start so long as there's decent money in it. People become entrepreneurs for all kinds of reasons, but I also know that many more people find even more reasons *not* to become an entrepreneur. This book is all about removing the barriers people put between themselves and their dreams, and helping you see the opportunities that are all around you. There is no reason why you can't start a business that will change your life.

Who is this book for?

I honestly believe that anyone can make £1 million, even £100 million. That doesn't mean to say that everyone *should* make a million. Many businesses will find their natural size with much lower turnovers, and many of those businesses are run by talented, dynamic and contented people who get a kick out of working for themselves. As far as I'm concerned, that's still a successful business. As Bob Dylan famously said, 'A man is a success if he gets up in the morning and gets to bed at night, and in between he does what he wants to do.'

Most successful entrepreneurs start a series of businesses before they start the one that makes them wealthy. This book will help you see your enterprise as a stepping stone in your career, either as you grow your first business or as you transfer the knowledge and skills you gain from your first business on to your second. The insights this book shares can just as easily be applied to small businesses as they can to ventures where the founders have very ambitious targets.

But this is also a book for someone who has never thought of starting a business before, perhaps someone who's looking at the shelves in a bookshop hoping to find a career manual or guide that will get them out of a rut. The techniques I describe are designed to be used by people unfamiliar with jargon and traditional business practice, and they will help take you from having an idle notion to a concrete plan for success.

I'm going to make a bold claim: this book is also for you if you earn less than £30,000 a year and want to earn more. I'm convinced that if you jack in your unrewarding job and follow the advice in this book, there's nothing to stop you earning more than that next year. You'll work harder than you've ever worked in your life, but not only will you be starting an amazing adventure, you will learn skills that will transform your career. You'll start to understand things about business that will enable you to earn good money regardless of what's happening in the economy, or if your employer goes bust or your sector is outsourced to cheaper companies overseas.

What this book isn't, though, is a Get Rich Quick book. It *is* possible to get rich in a very short space of time, but it's usually a fluke and not something you can properly teach. Through case studies from my own career and other entrepreneurs I have met – most of whom are not household names – I want to show that it's possible for anyone to acquire the basic insights and strategies for starting and growing a business.

Whether you're working on your own or as part of a small team, this book will help you plan a route through the early days of a business and get you on the road to business success. If you want to start a business that you will run for the rest of your career, or you want to start something you can sell for a large lump sum in the not-too-distant future, then you'll find plenty here to help you reach your goals.

What is an entrepreneur?

When I was a kid, no one had ever heard of the word 'entrepreneur' in Clydebank where I grew up. I was in my thirties when I first heard the word while I was trying to arrange a loan for several hundred thousand pounds from a bank manager who thought I was too big a risk. 'The problem with entrepreneurs,' he said, 'is that they just don't understand how the system works.' In fact, just about everything he had to say about entrepreneurs started with the words 'The problem with them is…' I didn't really know what he was talking about, but I got the impression that entrepreneurs were seen as troublemakers by the establishment. It was only when I got home and looked it up in the dictionary that I realised that I was one.

The dictionary told me the word is made up of the French words for entering and taking, and I thought that was pretty appropriate – you enter an industry and you take the profits. Business is just common sense – if you buy bananas for 50p and sell them for £1, you've made a profit. If you can grasp that, then you've got the makings of an entrepreneur.

Entrepreneurs come in all shapes and sizes. Some of them are incredibly competitive, some are dogged and hard-working, some of them are cavalier risk-takers, some of them are creative geniuses, while a few are visionaries and others opportunists. Some are dyslexic, some have PhDs, some are very upper crust, but most have pretty ordinary backgrounds. Some were teenage wunderkinds, some were late-starters like me. In my book, anyone who gets off their sofa and gives it a go is an entrepreneur.

I've found that most entrepreneurs fall into one of two camps: those who build up a business and can't imagine ever doing anything else because they love it so much, and those whose ambition is to create so much value in a business that they can then either pay someone else to run it for them or sell it for a lot of money. I certainly fall into the second category, but I know a lot of people in the first category who have a fantastic lifestyle working for themselves.

There is also a growing band of social entrepreneurs who start businesses for the greater good. The late Anita Roddick was one of the pioneers of social entrepreneurism, as she used profits from the Body Shop to support poor communities around the world and invested in things like recyclable packaging when other retailers hadn't heard of such innovations. It didn't stop her becoming a very wealthy woman. Using the same disciplines that make ventures profitable, social entrepreneurs run their businesses to benefit others and plough their profits back into their venture. Social entrepreneurs are responsible for some of the most exciting new businesses I know of. In fact, just about the best entrepreneur I know is a guy called Magnus MacFarlane-Barrow. He runs a charity called Scottish International Relief with the same focus and determination that chief executives run their companies in the commercial sector, and he has done things with a limited budget that larger organisations fail to achieve with much more money.

I've worked with many of the most successful entrepreneurs of my generation on TV shows like *Dragons' Den, Mind of a Millionaire, Fortune* and *Britain's Rich List: Giving It Away* and although we're all different, we probably share a few key traits: we take responsibility for our actions, we are a pretty principled bunch (contrary to popular belief, very few of us are ruthless), we love what we do, we're open to possibilities, and we are extremely hard-working. Anyone hoping that reading a book is a substitute for hard graft can put this back on the shelf now.

What is in this book?

I don't know about you, but I am bored with business manuals that tell you about the struggle Edison had getting the light bulb made, or Dyson had proving his cyclone cleaner was better than the vacuum cleaner. Through my public speaking and TV work, I meet a lot of people at all stages of running a business, from serial entrepreneur millionaires to first-timers working on the kitchen table. I've asked ten of them to share their stories for this book. Part of the reason I do so much public speaking –

apart from the fee, of course, which pays for a few treats – is to meet other people in business, as I learn something from everyone I meet. Sometimes I learn what *not* to do, but I learn nonetheless. So the case studies I've included here aren't the usual suspects; they're profiles of people in business today who are doing remarkable things that we can all learn from. As you'll see, we each have different skills, different attitudes and different advice.

A lot of new businesses fail in the first couple of years, and I'm pretty sure I know why, so this book is designed to alert you to common mistakes and to steer you clear of trouble. By arming you with the tools and techniques that can make your business profitable, this book will help you anticipate and deal with problems that often trip up new ventures. That said, you can only really learn about business by being in business. A book can't teach you everything you'll ever need to know – I firmly believe that only experience can do that – but it can get you started and over some of the hurdles that new businesses frequently encounter.

> ❛ *You can only learn about business by being in business.* ❜

Anyone can do it

When I started in business, I didn't have any money, any useful contacts or a track record. All I did was work hard to stockpile a bit of cash, look around for opportunities and reach for the Yellow Pages when I needed a phone number – and there's nothing to stop you doing exactly the same. You don't need to invent anything, you don't need to be 'first to market', you don't even need to do anything unique. You just need a bit of common sense and a lot of dedication.

I started my first business with £450, and when I sold it for £28,000 a few years later I had already started my next one. I sold my second business for £46 million. I can't promise that this book will make you a millionaire, but if you're smart, and you keep looking for opportunities, the skills you learn here will help you make your fortune.

What are you waiting for? It's time to wake up and change your life!

My CV

1964 I left school at 15 with no qualifications and joined the Royal Navy.

1968 I was dishonourably discharged for attempting to throw my commanding officer overboard.

1968–78 I trained as an agricultural fitter and welder, and started a series of dead-end jobs around Britain – bar work, driving taxis, repairing farm machinery, selling ice creams on the beach.

1978–79 I worked night shifts in a bakery to save up a deposit to buy a house. I made money on the side selling loaves from the bakery door to door. I also bought cars at auction, repaired them and sold them for a profit.

1979 My first business started when I bought a second-hand ice-cream van for £450. I looked up 'Ice Cream Suppliers' in the Yellow Pages and started selling ice creams at the weekend. As soon as it was clear I could make money, I quit my job at the bakery.

1980–85 Duncan's Super Ices expanded to include six vans and lucrative concessions in local parks, producing a turnover of £350,000 pa. I used some of the profits to buy terraced houses that I let out to DHSS tenants.

1984 The government passed new legislation that guaranteed payment for care of the elderly. I decided this was a sure-fire way to make money and started researching the care-home market. I was so appalled at dormitory accommodation where residents were forced to use commodes that I decided to build a nursing home with en-suite facilities from scratch. I sold the terraced houses and used cash from the ice-cream business to buy a plot of land. I then sold every-thing I had – my car, my TV, even my house – to secure a mortgage to build my first nursing home. I also sold Duncan's Super Ices for £28,000.

1986–91 Quality Care Homes expanded steadily, building nine homes in our first five years.

1992 Quality Care Homes was floated on the stock exchange. The company was valued at £18 million, making my personal wealth £12 million.

1993 I injured my leg in a skiing accident and started using a local gym to restore my fitness. I decided I could build a better gym.

1995 The government introduced new legislation guaranteeing payment for nursery education. I invested £2 million and launched a new business in the day nursery sector called Just Learning Ltd.

1996–2003 In addition to running my own companies, I worked as a non-executive director for a range of businesses from a radio station to sheltered housing.

1997 I opened the first Bannatyne's Health Club.

1997 I sold Quality Care Homes for £46 million.

1997–2007 Bannatyne Fitness expanded to become the UK's largest independent fitness chain.

2001 Just Learning Ltd was operating twenty day nurseries, and I sold it for £22 million.

2003 I was asked to take part in a new TV show called *Dragons' Den* featuring entrepreneurs trying to raise money for new ventures. Several other TV shows followed.

2006 I published my autobiography, *Anyone Can Do It: My Story*, which became a *Sunday Times* bestseller.

2007 Bannatyne Fitness acquired a chain of health clubs from Hilton hotels for £92 million.

2007 The *Sunday Times* Rich List estimated my wealth at £200 million.

2008 I founded the Bannatyne Charitable Trust to support causes close to my heart.

2008 The *Sunday Times* Rich List estimated my wealth at £310 million.

1 Removing the barriers

**When I give speeches, there's usually a question-and-answer
session afterwards, and virtually every time someone stands
up and says, 'It's OK for you to say that anyone can make a
million, but I can't do it because...' This chapter is all about
the 'because's. Sometimes I can spend half an hour with people
going through the reasons why they think they can't do what I
have done, and as soon as I've persuaded them the barriers
they're putting between themselves and their business don't
really exist, they find another 'because'.**

I thought twice about including this chapter – after all, many readers
will be itching to get to the 'how to make a million' bit – but the truth is,
you will come across all sorts of hurdles when starting a business. Even if
you're confident at the moment, the day may come when your confidence gets knocked and these imaginary barriers suddenly erect themselves right in front of you. They can make you consider quitting when
there really isn't any reason to. In the rest of the book, we'll deal with the
real problems you'll face, but right now I want to eliminate the imaginary
ones that might stop you from taking the plunge.

1 I don't have the time

When people tell me this, I ask them what they watched on TV last night, and more often than not, they give me a list of programmes. The simplest way to get more time in your life is to get rid of your TV. I'm not advocating giving up TV for ever – after all, I wouldn't want you to miss anything I was in – but if you're really serious about making this the year you start a business, put it in the loft or the shed for a year. Better yet, sell it and use the money to help get your business off the ground – you can always buy a bigger one when your new business starts making money.

When I was in the process of opening my first nursing home, I sold everything I had to raise the money I needed, and that included my TV. I'm so glad I got rid of it as it meant I was completely focused on starting my business. It also meant I had time to do up my house, which in turn meant I could sell it for a decent profit that I was then able to plough into the business. If I'd had a TV, I can honestly say I might not have had the career I've had. So ask yourself this: when you're on your deathbed, are you going to wish you'd watched more TV? Thought not. But you might well wish you'd made more of your life.

Of course, people have very serious commitments – raising a family, working long hours to pay for that family, caring for relatives – but I bet if you sat down with your diary and made a list of everything you do each week, you could find an hour here or there. And if you can just move a few appointments around, you might be able to create an entire free afternoon. At the early stages of a business, you don't need much time – a few hours checking out the competition, or a few hours doing a rough estimate of the costs is all it takes. If you plan a gradual transition from your current life to your new life as an entrepreneur, you can actually get a lot done each week.

If you're still having trouble finding the time, try this: keep a really detailed diary of your life for just one week. Make a note of everything you do, hour by hour. Find out how much time you spend commuting, shopping or ferrying the kids around and then see what you can ditch:

supermarkets deliver these days, so that saves a couple of hours; perhaps your kids could walk or cycle to their karate class, which might give you another hour. And do you really need to mow the lawn every week? Does it matter if your house isn't as clean as it used to be?

Look at all your commitments – perhaps you've taken on some extra responsibilities at work, or you're involved in the PTA or the residents' association – and see which you can step back from.

If you really want to start a business, you'll find the time.

2   I don't have any money

There is a myth that starting a business costs a lot of money. Some businesses do, but most entrepreneurs I know invested less than £10,000 in their first venture, and a whole bunch of those got going with far less. I started my first business by buying a second-hand ice-cream van for £450. I spent another £50 on stock and started selling ice creams. Some businesses don't cost anything at all, and if you can start your first business on a shoestring, you build up credibility with banks and investors for your next venture.

The average amount of cash Britons have in savings accounts is a whopping £18,705 (source: NS&I Savings Survey 2007). Although this is skewed by people with hundreds of thousands squirrelled away, most of us have access to a bit of cash. The same survey shows that 23 per cent have less than £1000 put aside, but I can think of plenty of businesses that can be started for less than a grand (see the list on page 24 for some ideas). And these are all ventures you might well be able to sell within a few years for tens of thousands of pounds – more than enough to start a much bigger business. You may have to amend your dreams to fit your circumstances in the short term, but lack of funds shouldn't stop you making your move.

Costs in any start-up venture can be kept to a minimum by hard work and common sense. There are several mechanisms that new businesses can use to reduce outgoings – such as arranging 60 days' credit to pay your suppliers but getting your customers to pay straight away – that make it quite possible to start small and build up quickly.

If you only need a few hundred or a few thousand quid to get off the mark, then perhaps you can do a bit of overtime and stockpile some cash. A second job can really increase your ability to save, as not only are you earning more, but you're going out less. Bar work is a great way to do this: the hours allow you to keep your existing job, and you can still hang about in your local and chat to your mates. And if you have a look round your house, you can probably find plenty of items – gadgets, books, CDs, even cars – that you can sell on eBay to raise a bit of cash.

If you need more than a couple of grand to get started, there are a number of ways you can finance your new business. If you have a brilliant business idea, and you can prove that you are the right person to lead that business, then there's probably a financial institution or an investor who will back you. Some businesses might even be eligible for grants and interest-free loans, and later in the book I'll introduce you to all the different sources of finance.

Homeowners are usually able to extend their mortgages, and adding an extra £10,000 to your home loan may have less of an impact on your outgoings than you think. At an interest rate of 7 per cent, on an interest-only basis, it would only set you back £58 a month (or around £72 on a repayment basis) if you paid it back over 25 years. I would never advocate equity release for frivolous purchases, but investing some of your wealth in yourself rather than your property makes good sense to me.

Tenants can borrow too. Unsecured personal loans of up to £25,000 are offered by most lenders if you've got a good credit rating. If you haven't, you might have to pay a higher interest rate, or borrow slightly less, but you should still be able to borrow some of what you'll need. My back was against the wall when I opened my first nursing home, and I borrowed an additional £30,000 on credit cards – probably £90,000 in today's money – and juggled until I could make the payments. My fellow Dragon James Caan tells me he also maxed out his overdrafts to get his first venture off the ground. This should probably be your last resort, but if you really believe in your business and, crucially, you really believe in your figures, then you should feel confident borrowing against future profits. When we come to the chapter on raising finance, you'll see that I'm a big fan of getting into debt.

Finally, if you can't get backing, then maybe you can scale down your launch, build up a track record and then seek investment later. By the end of this book, you'll have a clear plan of your launch and how to tailor your business to the funds available. Lack of money is rarely a good enough reason not to give a strong idea a fighting chance, and in my experience people would rather blame a lack of funds than a lack of belief or desire.

Ten businesses that can be started for under £1000

1   House-cleaning

2   Driving a taxi (if you already have a car. If not, why not hire someone else's cab and drive it when they're not using it?)

3   Setting up as a consultant in your existing profession

4   Trading on eBay

5   A market stall

6   A sandwich round

7   Gardening

8   Alternative therapies practitioner

9   Party planner

10 Painting and decorating

I bet if you took 15 minutes, you could come up with another ten – there are thousands of these sorts of business ideas out there.

3　I can't afford a drop in salary

For most people, the thought of leaving behind a regular salary for a career where the returns can't be guaranteed is unnerving. That's understandable, but some people become so focused on the insecurity that they lose perspective.

For starters, they don't realise how insecure their current jobs are. Between March and June 2007, 120,000 people were made redundant in the UK according to the Office of National Statistics. That's in just three months. With many more people employed casually or on a contract basis than ever before, increasing numbers of Britons are realising just how fragile employment can be. However, there is an upside: with a pay-off in their pocket, workers who are made redundant are often in an excellent position to strike out on their own. I hear stories all the time about the founders of new companies who had been thinking about starting the business for years, but who had needed the shock of redundancy to jolt them into action.

If you really want job security, then the best way to get it is to acquire the skills and acumen that will see your earning power survive downturns in the economy, outsourcing overseas or a technological innovation that leaves you surplus to requirements. The best way I know of doing that is by understanding how businesses are run and obtaining the skills to steer them through the tough times. Nothing teaches you how to adapt to change like starting a business. What people often fail to ask themselves is, 'Can I afford *not* to take a drop in salary?'

On a practical level, there's plenty you can do to get yourself into better financial shape, which will enable you to take a temporary drop in salary in your stride. Not all of my suggestions will work for everyone, but I've found that most people can find ways to cope by using a combination of these methods:

1　**Save up.** One of the simplest things to do is to stockpile as much as you can before you leave your job, and if you can, do overtime or get a second job. Maybe you could even think about letting a room.

You can earn up to £4250 a year from a lodger under the government's Rent-a-Room scheme without having to pay tax on the income.

2 **Reduce your outgoings.** It may be possible to remortgage to a better rate for the next couple of years. Or if you have debts, perhaps consolidating them with one lender would mean there'd be a couple of hundred pounds less a month you'd need to find. Switch to a cheaper provider for your phone and utilities, and stop paying for unnecessary insurance and payment protection policies.

3 **Go without.** Never a popular suggestion, but it's amazing how much we buy that we don't really need. Last year's fashions will have to do. You're not going to have time to play with gadgets, watch DVDs or go on holiday, so that could save you thousands. Ditch your TV subscription and cancel those direct debits for things you barely use. I promise you won't miss them: you're going to be far too busy.

The one thing that really annoys me is when people tell me they can't raise the cash and then promptly get out a packet of cigarettes. If you smoke a packet a day, you are throwing away nearly £2000 a year, ruining your health and – in my opinion – failing to show the kind of common sense that makes a good entrepreneur. Give up.

If you start making all these changes now, by the time you're ready to start your business in a few months' time, you might have already built up a cushion that will insulate you from worrying too much about money.

4 It's not just the loss of income; I can't risk throwing away my career

This is another very understandable concern, but again I think it's a risk people get out of proportion. However, it probably explains why so many millionaires in the UK left school without any qualifications: people who feel they've got nothing to lose will risk it all. The prospect of a decent career has deterred many people from becoming entrepreneurs.

What I can't – and won't – do is tell you that there isn't a risk to leaving your job, but I can tell you that if you don't leave your job, your dreams of starting a business (and perhaps of becoming a millionaire) are unlikely to amount to much. The crucial thing is to assess the size of the risk, and I bet with a little level-headed thinking you'll see it's not such a risky thing to do after all.

So you need to ask yourself what's the worst thing that could happen if you walked away from your career for six months or a year? Women do it all the time when they take extended maternity leave, and although some have claimed this has hindered their career, there are very few who wish they hadn't taken the time out to have children. It's much the same way with a business: if you do end up compromising your career slightly, at least you won't be sitting there when you're approaching retirement wondering, What if?

However, the chances are that taking a career break to start a business will give your career a sizeable boost. Not only will you learn skills and insights that will be valuable to any future employer, but you will have proved yourself to be hard-working, passionate and pro-active. You'll stand out a mile from the hordes of clock-watchers who apply for most positions, and I can bet you that the first thing you'll be asked about at any future job interview will be your time as an entrepreneur.

People worry about explaining their absence from their career on their CVs. I always find this surprising: I can't think why you would want to hide your entrepreneurial streak from a future employer. But if you're really concerned, fudging a few leaving and starting dates might allow you to hide any perceived blemish on your corporate record.

I really don't think anyone should do that, though. Not only might you be found out (and that's no way to impress your new boss), but we no longer live in a society where people leave school and expect to work for the same company until they draw their pensions. Careers are becoming less linear and more and more people are having what's known as a 'portfolio career'. That means taking their skills from sector to sector, from job to job, and they often wear two or three hats at once. The papers are full of articles about employees taking sabbaticals and career breaks, and I think the concept of work–life balance is now far better understood by many employers. A slightly unusual CV is actually very ordinary these days.

5 My partner doesn't support me

This is a serious stumbling block. Starting a business is such a massive commitment that it's very difficult to do it without the support of those closest to you. I once received a letter from a woman telling me the only thing holding her back was the fact that her boyfriend didn't believe in her. I wrote back and said, 'Dump him'! I wasn't being entirely flippant. In some ways, it's easier to start a business when you're single, but I also know that the support of a partner can be the one thing that helps to keep you going.

You need to find out exactly why your partner is reluctant to support you. Do they not want you to risk the money, or perhaps they're worried you won't be around so much to help with the kids? It might even be because they don't believe in your idea as much as you do, or worse, perhaps they don't believe in you.

Once you know what their objection is, you can offer reassurance. You can agree a limit between you for the amount of money and time you will invest in the idea. You can use the arguments at the beginning of this chapter to persuade them that the risk is perceived rather than real, and that the real risk lies in not giving it a go.

Of course, your partner's doubts about your business might be well founded. If you discuss it together in detail, they may become convinced of its worth, or you may be persuaded of some previously unseen flaw. It may also help to find a way of involving your partner in the venture – what skills do they have that can help move you forward? Sometimes people are worried about being left out or left behind, and you need to acknowledge that your bold move into business might make them feel vulnerable on several levels. What if your new life is more exciting? What if you meet interesting people and your partner feels dull by comparison? What if money's tight? Before you can reassure them, you'll need to know why they're feeling insecure, so now's the time for an honest and open discussion.

Finally, if the problem is that they don't believe in you, then you have to be determined to prove them wrong. Many a fortune has been made by entrepreneurs who were determined to show doubters what they were made of, and I'd definitely include myself in that category.

6 I don't have the experience

Neither did I. Neither did Alan Sugar, or Gordon Ramsay, or most of the Dragons. We all started somewhere. One of the most important things I'd like to get across in this book is that you very rarely go from starting your first business to becoming incredibly wealthy in just a few years. Most entrepreneurs started a series of businesses – some of which will have flopped – before they started the one that made them a fortune.

As I've said before, you can only really learn about business by being in business. The truth is, you could read every book ever written on how to start a business, but until you start one yourself, you will never know what it's like. So get out there, discover the skills you'll need to make a success, and put a couple of years' experience in the bank. Your ambitions may change once you've got your first business under your belt. You'll also grow in confidence, and the time will come when you'll be capable of making a success of any business.

The only way you can overcome this reservation is by taking those first steps.

7 I don't have the qualifications

Usually, the people I speak to think there are two types of qualification they lack: a) some kind of business management diploma, and b) something specific to the industry they want to enter. I tell them that I still don't have a single qualification to my name. I've never taken book-keeping classes, let alone sat accountancy exams, but I can read and prepare a balance sheet. Over the years, I've made money in residential care for the elderly, day care for toddlers and health clubs – but I've never had a qualification in any of those fields.

All it takes to run a business is common sense. Throughout this book, there is advice on how to do everything from filling in VAT returns to dealing with health and safety legislation. One of the first things I discovered when I started in business is that the government produces a leaflet for everything. Absolutely everything. Whatever sector your business is in, whatever size your company is, and no matter what taxes and levies you become liable for, there is a leaflet and a helpline. Just take your time to read them and not only will you save on professional administration costs, but you will get to know your business inside out. It takes a little time, but it doesn't take qualifications.

If you're still daunted, then you can always employ external accountants, bookkeepers or lawyers to deal with these hassles for you. If you pay a monthly retainer, it might only cost you a few hundred pounds a month – not a lot for a successful business, but a bit of a drain on a small one.

Sector-specific qualifications in certain professions can also be bought in or employed directly. For instance, I needed to employ nurses in my care homes, but I didn't need to be one. And the same is true for most businesses that employ qualified staff.

> **‘ *All it takes to run a business is common sense.* ’**

Top five things people are most afraid of in business

1 VAT returns

They're really not that difficult; you simply keep a record of the VAT you've charged on your goods and services, and the amount you've been charged on the goods and services you've bought in. The rest is simple arithmetic. Just make sure you keep good records. And you don't have to do all the paperwork straight away. You'll only have to register for VAT if your turnover is over £67,000, so don't worry about it yet, and please don't use it as an excuse not to grow your business.

2 Spreadsheets

Learning to create a spreadsheet is a very valuable skill for an entrepreneur. If you've never used one before, ask a friend for a tutorial, or follow the manual that came when you bought the software. Alternatively, go to an evening class or try the tutorials available online. I found a pretty good one at www.spreadsheet123.com, but there are loads of others out there.

3 Pay roll

Being responsible for employees' salaries, tax and National Insurance payments is daunting for many. However, the Inland Revenue produce a very clear leaflet and have a well-staffed helpline if you have any questions. As soon as you've done it once, you'll not worry about doing it again.

4 Incorporation

Incorporating your business to become a limited company involves a fair bit of paperwork, and first-timers worry they're making a commitment to file reports for life and take on responsibilities as directors. It's really not so difficult, and there's a helpline at Companies House that can talk you through every step of the application process. Research by the

Department for Business, Enterprise and Regulatory Reform shows that on average business founders spend five hours a week dealing with red tape. Their research also showed that most non-entrepreneurs assume the red-tape burden would be at least ten hours a week – enough to put most of them off starting a business. I promise you, you'll learn what you need to learn as you go along.

5 Failure

I wonder if this is the real reason why most people don't start their own businesses. A lot of people don't want to have to face family and friends who were always sceptical of their chances of success. They've probably heard the statistic that 50 per cent of businesses fail in their first two years, but this statistic is usually based on the closure of business bank accounts, *not* the closure of businesses. If you remove the number of businesses that change bank accounts when introductory deals run out, or the number of businesses that are wound up because the founder took up a lucrative job offer, or started another business, the so-called failure figure drops dramatically. Barclays' New Business division estimates that the number of businesses that close because of 'external financial stress', i.e. owing money, is just 12 per cent in the first year, and 31 per cent within two years. If you follow the advice in this book, your exposure to failure will be reduced further.

And let's not forget, no matter what happens to your business, you will have succeeded in acquiring skills and knowledge that will increase your earning power and give you the confidence to start another business. It's true, if you don't give it a go you'll never fail, but if you don't accept the possibility of failure, you'll never get the chance to succeed.

Name: Alexander Amosu **Age**: 32
Job: CEO, Amosu Luxury Ltd
Qualifications: 4 GCSEs, left university in final year
www.amosu.co.uk

I started my first proper business when I was 19, but I was making money long before that. I've always said that if you dropped me in the middle of Kosovo or Kazakhstan with nothing in my pockets, I could find a way of making money within a couple of hours.

At 14, I organised a five-a-side football competition at school. I never got picked to play, so I thought if I started my own competition, I could make sure I got a game. I went to the headmistress and told her what I wanted to do. When she gave her OK, I went to the school library and photocopied some flyers that said we wanted to find out who the best players were. It was £5 per player, and a minimum of seven players per team. I then went out and bought some medallions for £2, a trophy for £5 and persuaded the canteen manager to use the leftovers to provide the food for free. Like so many businesses, I had started out trying to fulfil a need, and along the way had spotted an opportunity to make money. In the end I forgot to enter my own team, so I refereed the matches, and that day I went home with £1,200.

The thing about me is that I don't ask for permission to do anything. I didn't tell the headmistress I was going to charge for entry, probably because I knew she would say no. These days, my business customises luxury mobile phones, and we have just produced a diamond-encrusted Motorola and Apple iPhone. I have a lot of advisers now, and my lawyer asked if I'd got permission from the mobile manufacturers to luxurify their phones. Of course I hadn't. If I had gone to them, they would have said no because it's the easiest answer to give, and then if they had a problem with it *after* I had customised their phones, they could complain. One of the mobile manufacturers did call me in for a meeting, but only to offer me a contract as their exclusive partner for luxury customisations! I know I would never have got that if I'd asked for permission first.

Although I was born in England, I grew up in Nigeria until I was 11, when I moved back to live with my grandmother in a two-bedroom council flat in Kilburn. My brother and I slept in the living room and things were very tight. If I wanted anything, I knew it would be down to me to go out and get it. It made me very self-reliant, even after my parents came to Britain when I was 15.

After the football tournament, I started a mobile DJ business with my cousins. We all put in £100 to buy the equipment and then charged £250 to DJ at house parties. But the speakers were so big that I needed to buy a car to move them around. The car I wanted cost £2500, so I calculated that I could get the money together in a month if I worked nine to six at the electrical shop Tandy's, and then from seven until midnight at Pizza Hut. I believe anyone can do what I did – get a couple of jobs, work flat out for a month and get enough money together to start a small venture. The car meant we could make even more money from the DJing, but I kept a weekend job at Tandy's, which gave me about £500 a month, and I used that money to try out various little schemes, like buying and selling at boot sales. Some months I'd make money, some months I would lose the lot, but I knew at the end of the month I'd have another £500 to play with. I suppose it was a bit like Lewis Hamilton, who spent his teenage years go-karting in preparation for Formula One. All those little businesses I started were my apprenticeship, and I made the most of living at home and not having any financial commitments. I made a lot of mistakes, but it didn't matter because I was so young, and now when I start a business I think I have a 70 per cent chance of success because I've already made my mistakes.

My family is Nigerian, and it's part of our culture that you want your kids to be a lawyer or a doctor. Being in a profession is a kind of status symbol, and my parents didn't see my schemes as the start of a career. My dad wanted me to be an aeronautical engineer, and even though I didn't know what one was, I went to university to become one. After my first year, I transferred to a sound engineering course.

All the time I was at university, I carried on with the mobile DJ business and organised university and club parties at Christmas, Easter and Valentine's, but I also started what I call my first proper business while I was studying. My aunt was heavily pregnant and couldn't bend to do the housework, so I did her cleaning for her. I did such a good job that she gave me £20. I thought there must be other people who needed a cleaner, so I designed a flyer, distributed 1000 of them around our neighbourhood and, to my amazement, someone called up. When I turned up on her doorstep, however, she wasn't sure about letting some kid in. I completely understood her reservations, so I went home and put on my dad's suit. I asked my mum for a copy of my passport and a reference, and I also asked my aunt to write me a reference. I went straight back to my potential client and told her that she could read the references, she could see from my passport that I was who I said I was, and if anything got stolen, this was her security. I also made her an offer: I will clean your house free for a week, and if at the end of the week you are happy, then I charge £20 an hour for a minimum of two hours; and if you are not happy, then it won't have cost you anything. So she said 'yes', and in typical Amosu style, I took off the suit there and then and started cleaning: I had my first contract.

I got in touch with the Prince's Trust, and they helped me write a business plan for my cleaning business. I think they were very impressed that a young person not only wanted to start a cleaning business but already had some clients, and they gave me a grant for £2000. I used the money to advertise in the Yellow Pages and create a website, and the business grew to 14 clients, half of which were commercial clients, and I employed two people I'd got from the job centre. I had a turnover of £2000 a month. It was the first time I'd had to keep proper accounts, and I quickly learnt that sitting behind a desk and dealing with paperwork is not one of my strengths. I'm good at coming up with ideas, setting things in motion and building them up. Knowing your strengths and understanding your weaknesses is a very important part of being successful. Wherever I can, I now employ people to do the jobs I know I'm not good at.

At 24, I believed I had spotted a massive opportunity to make a business out of mobile ring tones, and so I quit university and gave the cleaning business up. It could have been a really big business – people will always need cleaners – and if I'd stuck with it, I think it could be turning over £100,000 a month now, but the people I sold the business to ran it into the ground. It was still the right decision, though, as I was correct about the ring tones: my new business turned over £1.6 million in its first year and was sold for a lot more.

What's the best advice you've ever had? My mum always told me that if there's something you want to do in life, don't let anybody stop you. If there's something I really want, I don't care how many people tell me I can't do it, I'll find a way.

What do you wish you'd known from the start? You know, I think because I had all those ventures when I was young, I'd figured out what I needed to know about starting a business.

What's the one thing you'd say to someone starting their first business? Know your strengths and play to them. Find out what your weaknesses are and find a way of plugging those gaps in your business. If you're forced to do something that you're not good at, it will drive you into the ground.

2 The idea

This chapter is about finding an idea for a business that is capable of making money. On *Dragons' Den*, we see lots of great ideas but not many good businesses, and it's often clear that people have wasted time and money on a pipe dream. You might already have an idea for the sort of business you'd like to run, but are you sure there's profit in your idea?

When I decided that I would stop being a beach bum and start becoming a millionaire, I didn't know what sort of business I would start, but I knew that I would know the right opportunity when it came my way. Although I had no previous affinity with the ice-cream business, residential care homes, day nurseries or health clubs, when I found an opportunity that I was sure would make money, I changed direction and went for it.

There are thousands upon thousands of ideas out there waiting to be turned into businesses, and once you start looking for opportunities, they are not hard to find.

PART 1 – Finding the idea

Where do ideas come from?

Ideas for new businesses broadly fall into three categories – those that solve a problem, those that copy another business and those spawned from genuine innovation. In my experience, precious few successful businesses fall into the last category, and yet I meet a lot of people who tell me they would start a business if only they could come up with a blinding idea. They seem surprised when I tell them I've never had an original idea for a business in my life.

Problem-solving businesses

I call these Wouldn't It Be Good businesses, because we can probably all recall a time when we've said, 'Wouldn't it be good if I could just buy/use/get some product or service that doesn't exist?' When real entrepreneurs find a gap in the market like that, their brains start whirring and they start to find out if there's a market in the gap.

Believe it or not, a woman once approached me with an idea for a business that she said solved a real problem. 'Wouldn't it be good,' she said, 'if when you stop at traffic lights someone would come along and sell you a bottle of water?' I had to tell her that this wasn't a business, it was just an idea, and an exceedingly bad idea at that.

However, sometimes we do encounter problems that alert us to real opportunities. When I had trouble getting day-care places for my kids, I realised there was a market to start a children's day nursery – and this was despite the fact that there were already ten such nurseries in our town. When I broke my leg and needed to drive for half an hour to a gym with the right equipment to rebuild the muscles, I realised there was an opportunity to open a health club nearer my home.

Many of the best business ideas we've seen on *Dragons' Den* have been ones that address a real need. Sometimes these are just slight improvements on existing products or services; sometimes they involve inventions and revolutionary gadgets – so long as we can see that they solve real problems experienced by most people, we'll give these businesses consideration because the best reason to start a business is because the customer *needs* it.

Most social entrepreneurs seek to launch problem-solving businesses where the need is overwhelming. Whether they end up making a profit is often incidental to whether they make a difference, but the growth of ethical businesses and green investment funds suggests that there will increasingly be profit in this area.

If you already know what your business will be, then ask yourself who needs it. How do you make your potential customers' lives easier or better? If you can come up with a good answer, then you're heading in the right direction.

Copycat ideas

As I've said, when I opened my first children's day nursery, it wasn't the only one in my neighbourhood. Nor was I the only guy selling ice cream in Stockton in the 1980s. I certainly wasn't the first person to open a health club, and Richard Branson wasn't the first guy to start an airline, or a record company, or to offer a mobile phone service. There's no shame in copying someone else's business.

However, I wouldn't be proud of my businesses if I didn't think I had improved on the one I was copying. My day nurseries had facilities others didn't offer – bathrooms next to the classrooms so children didn't need accompanying to the loo, ample parking for parents, different play areas for different age groups – and my nursing homes were among the first in the country to provide private rooms with en-suite toilets. This significantly improved the quality of care we could offer, and lifted us above the competition. James Dyson famously made his fortune by making a cleaner that worked better than Hoover's vacuum technology. When you study a business you're thinking of copying, you should always think about how you can make it better. I can't stress how important this is: not only will it motivate you to prove that you're the best in your field, but it will enable you to overtake other companies in your sector.

Copying an idea doesn't necessarily mean you'll be successful, however. Just because one coffee shop is full, it doesn't automatically mean that there's enough custom to support a second one. The flip side of that is that if a coffee shop is empty, it doesn't always mean that there isn't a market for another one. You just need to work out why the existing one is empty, and if you then think you can open a better one, you have to judge if that will be enough to get the punters in.

Some of the best copycat ideas take a business that works in one location and transports it to a new area, which is what I did when I opened a health club in an area where there wasn't one. If you see a business thriving in another town that would work just as well in yours, then that's something to consider. You can also take a service or product and offer it to a new market, like taking beauty salons for women and starting an identical business aimed at the male-grooming market. Similarly, is there a business in the real world that would work online, or the other way round?

Genuine innovation

Every now and then, someone comes up with an idea for a product or service that we didn't know we needed but now can't live without. Things like computers and aeroplanes. No doubt when they were first suggested, the inventors' friends and families thought they were deluded. When these come along, they represent a massive opportunity, but in my experience with *Dragons' Den*, a new idea rarely makes a good new business. One woman asked us to invest in cardboard beach furniture: she thought it was a great idea because it could carry advertising. I thought it was a crap idea because you couldn't sit on it if you'd just come out of the sea!

Where to look for ideas

I reckon I spot around 20 opportunities a week that someone could make a viable business out of. Whether I'm in a shop and getting ideas about how to improve it, or reading something in a newspaper about a new trend, I see business ideas everywhere I go. If I get overcharged in a garage, I wonder why someone hasn't opened a more competitively priced garage in opposition. If I see something for sale on holiday that I've not seen in Britain, I wonder why someone hasn't started importing it. If I eat in a bad restaurant, I think there's an opportunity to start a rival, and if I eat in a good restaurant, I wonder if the owner has thought of franchising the operation. If you're still searching for a business idea, then here are my tips on where to look.

Watch the news

I got the idea to start a nursing home from watching the news. In the early 1980s, the government announced it was going to pay £140 a week per patient for residential care. Anyone watching the news that night could have said exactly what I said: 'If I had 50 residents, that means I'd have a guaranteed turnover of £7000 a week.' The nightly news is full of leads for potential businesses, whether it's a jokey piece about a new trend in Japan, a serious initiative about recycling or the introduction of Home Information Packs for house sellers that creates the need for a new service.

Successful entrepreneurs know that change creates opportunity. Whether that's legislative change, cultural change or climate change, these shifts require businesses and industries to change too. Often, existing businesses are slow to adapt, which means new operators who get their model right and who move quickly can make their mark.

What annoys you?

What would make your life easier? A cleaner? A personal shopper? Someone to do the school run? An easier commute? Wherever there's a problem, there might be a solution you can turn into a business. I got the idea to open a health club when I had to drive half an hour to find somewhere I could exercise my knee muscles after a skiing accident. I knew I couldn't be the only person who didn't want to drive for half an hour for an hour's work-out, so I opened a gym near my house. My first day-care nursery was opened because I couldn't find one locally that could take both my daughters at the same time, so I knew there had to be a need for more nurseries.

For the next couple of weeks, pay attention when friends and colleagues moan about something and see if there's anything that could be done to alleviate their inconvenience. Look around you for signs of discontent – in your local paper, in the queue at the post office – as it's usually the case that where there is dissatisfaction you will also find opportunity.

Read the financial pages

Every day, newspapers print information that's useful to aspiring entrepreneurs and sometimes it can be the tiniest piece of gossip that can spark an idea. By reading the financial pages regularly, you will not only become familiar with the language and practices of business, but over time you might spot trends, learn from other people's mistakes or find out about innovations before the wider public does. The financial pages also regularly profile successful entrepreneurs, who will inspire you and give you business models you can copy and modify.

Read the trade press

If you know you want to work in a certain industry, then bone up on what matters to that industry by reading the relevant trade magazine. What are the trends? Who's in difficulty? Who's leading the pack? Careful analysis of the landscape should help you find a path towards a profitable business.

Read the local paper

Not only do local papers have a Businesses for Sale section in their classifieds pages, but they are full of people experiencing problems. Local papers are where the nation moans the most, and if your neighbours are up in arms about poor facilities or poor services, you can devise all sorts of ideas for businesses that might solve some of their problems. You also find out what sorts of businesses are getting planning permission, or grants from the council. You might even come across a few useful names you could call for help in the future. If you want to start a business in a particular town, you should absolutely read that town's local press every week. And not just the paper – if there's an online forum or newsletter, you should be a regular visitor.

Of course, a careful reading of the Businesses for Sale listings arms you with all sorts of useful information. For starters, you might actually see a business you want to buy, but you might also start to see patterns – the sorts of businesses people are trying to bail out from, the kind of money needed to buy commercial leases, or which are the booming parts of town.

Look at your current job

Sometimes the best new businesses are started by people who already work in that industry. Is your current employer ignoring your customers' needs? Are they not responding quickly enough to innovation and change in your industry? Are they running out of ideas, or steam, or goodwill? Or perhaps they're wasting money and resources and becoming uncompetitive. If you can find a chink in your employer's armour, you may be very well placed to launch a rival – especially if you can take the best employees and clients with you.

Look at your interests

Think about the other areas of your life – your passions, hobbies and leisure activities. Is there an area in which you can claim to have some expertise or hard-won knowledge? Is there an area you may be better placed to exploit than the rest of us?

Listen to your friends

If you find yourself having the same conversation time and time again about the problems people are having with childcare, parking, housing, cleaning, shopping or whatever else, then it's quite likely someone should be seeing if a solution to those problems and inconveniences might be the start of a profitable business. That someone should be you.

Use your eyes

Take a walk around your neighbourhood and look at each and every single business – the big chains, the little operators, the nearly invisible businesses that just have a tiny sign above the bell. Ask yourself why they opened where they did, if they could be any busier, if they're offering the best service and the best price. Make a note of any business you think might be fun to work in. Think about who's missing a trick, who's turning customers away without really thinking about it. Ask yourself what you can improve on.

If you see a business that's doing spectacularly well, or spectacularly badly, ask yourself why. Applying a little common sense to the businesses that are around us can reveal all sorts of opportunities. For instance, no one likes queuing. Wherever you see a queue, you see a line of customers who might easily be persuaded to shop somewhere else.

I found my first hotel – Hotel Bannatyne in Darlington – by driving round my home town looking for something in which I could invest the money I'd made from selling my care-homes company. My wife and I turned our hunt for opportunities into day trips out: other couples visit stately homes or garden centres; we enjoy business, so that's what we did for fun.

Things to look for while you're on the road:

* **Queues** – either there's demand for a rival or someone's service could be fine-tuned.

* **What's missing?** Most towns have the same mix of businesses: shops, gyms, restaurants, cinemas, etc. What's missing in your town? If you can't think of an obvious reason why it's missing, then maybe there's an opportunity.

* **Who's in the neighbourhood?** If your neighbourhood is predominantly home to pensioners, you don't want to be opening a nightclub. But a home-help service might have plenty of waiting customers.

* **Who's in the wrong location?** Sometimes people start really good businesses in terrible locations. Could you move a struggling business to a new location and make it thrive?

* **Who hasn't updated their stock in a long time?** A business that hasn't moved with the times could be vulnerable if you opened an up-to-date rival.

PART 2 – Analysing the idea

Coming up with ideas is the easy bit. Whoever said success is 1 per cent inspiration and 99 per cent perspiration was right. Ideas are cheap – execution is everything.

At this stage I want you to use a little bit of quality control to check that your idea is worth taking further. Doing this early on can save you a lot of time and money down the line. People sometimes get so entranced by the big picture and their dreams of success that they overlook some of the basics. I've seen lots of entrepreneurs over the years who have had an idea, launched into it headlong, committed a lot of cash, and then refused to see sense precisely because they have already invested so much in their dream. Believe me, it's better to use a little common sense before you've wasted energy and cash. The purpose of this section of the book is to enable you to do what I call a fag-packet calculation of whether or not your idea is worth taking further – a snapshot of the likelihood of success.

Who else is doing it?

The first thing to check is if anyone else is already doing what you're thinking of starting. Just because you haven't heard of your rivals, it doesn't mean your potential customers haven't. I was once approached by a man from Bristol who wanted to start an air-conditioning business. He told me he didn't have any rivals as no one was offering air-conditioning systems in his town. So I went to Yell.co.uk, typed in 'air-conditioning' and 'Bristol' and it brought up ten results. He had wasted his time and I wasn't going to waste my money.

So how can you find out who's already offering the same or similar products and services? There are several things you can do:

Check your local phone directory. Think about where you would look to find the company you want to start and see who is advertising in that section. Then think about what other sections someone might list a similar business in: you could be looking up 'Garden Services', but you might find a rival in 'Landscaping Supplies'.

Google for similar companies. You may need to enter several variations of your search criteria, and it might be that your biggest rival is buried in an avalanche of results. Just because someone hasn't optimised their site for search engines this week, don't assume they won't have got their web strategy right by the time you launch. Make a note of every potential rival you find.

If you intend to sell a product, search for it on sites like eBay and Kelkoo. See how many people are offering what you intend to bring to the market, and see how much they are charging for it. How does your product compare? Can you compete with them on price?

Look at the ads in your local paper, or even in newsagents' windows. If you have a local chamber of commerce, phone them up and tell them you want to find someone who can supply the thing you intend to offer and see if they can give you the names of your rivals.

Send an email to everyone you know casually asking if anyone can recommend a good practitioner in the field you intend to enter. If they all email back and say, 'No, but if you find one, be sure to let me know,' then you should start to feel encouraged.

Finding a rival doesn't mean you should give up. Quite the contrary in fact, as competition can help you define where your business will fit into the marketplace. To do this, you need to get to know your rivals, and the best way to do this is to pretend to be a potential customer. Phone them up or visit them. Can they do everything you are thinking of doing? How good is their service? How do their products measure up? How keen are their prices?

One of the first things I did when I was looking to open my first care home was to visit all the existing care homes in the area. I pretended I was looking for a home for my mother – and I'm so glad that I wasn't: up to eight residents were sharing a room and having to use commodes because there weren't accessible toilets. I was horrified, but it told me exactly what I needed to be able to offer to attract residents: private rooms with en-suite bathrooms.

By checking out the competition, you might find that they've all failed to move with the times and would be vulnerable to a sharp new operator, or you might find that they do everything you were thinking of doing at a very competitive price. If you discover the former, that's fantastic, but if it's the latter, be prepared to walk away from your idea. However, it might be that they tell you they're flat out and have more orders than they can cope with, in which case you know there are people out there who want to buy whatever it is you intend to sell.

Finally, when you've identified your rivals, ask yourself why someone would choose to buy from you and not from them. What can you do differently? Consumers make choices based on:

* Price

* Convenience

* Location

* Quality

* Customer service

* Ethical considerations

If you can beat the competition on one (or ideally more) of those fronts, then it's worth pursuing your idea. If you can't, it's probably time to come up with another idea.

● ● ● ● ● **BANNATYNE'S BOOTCAMP** ● ● ● ● ●

Checking on the competition

1   Be their customer. Obviously this is easier if they don't know who you are (and if they do, send a friend), but it's an unmissable chance to see how they operate, and to check out their range and their customer service.

2   Join their mailing list. Most companies use a mailing list to tell customers about new products and special offers.

3   Set up a Google alert for them so you won't miss them if they make the news.

4   Hang out in chat rooms and online forums where your industry is discussed. Using a different name, you can float all sorts of suggestions about and see how others respond.

5   If they're a limited company, ask Companies House for the annual accounts they are obliged to lodge each year. If they're a plc, their accounts will be available from the stock exchange.

● ●

Who are your customers?

Never make the assumption that just because you'd like a cardboard deckchair or a home-maintenance service or even a reliable supply of tiddlywinks everyone else will. You need to establish that your business idea sounds as good to your potential customers as it does to you.

First of all, you need to think about what type of people your customers will be. Are you appealing to a technological elite? The skateboarding community? Or busy parents? Take a moment to think carefully about who will buy your product or service. Now think generally about how many of your potential customers you can reasonably reach. If you're thinking of opening a shop, you need to consider how many of your potential customers will walk past your front door each day; and if you're thinking about starting a website, you need to estimate how many of your target customers have internet access.

It can be very difficult to aim a new business at 'everyone'. It's much easier to have a meaningful connection with potential customers if you target your offering to a particular section of society. If you're successful, in time you can start seeking out a wider audience, but begin by giving some thought as to who your likeliest customers will be in your first year of trading.

Market research

Once you've worked out who your target customers are, you need to assess how many of them are likely to become actual customers. You've got to be realistic: people aren't going to drive 100 miles for a new product from a company they've never heard of.

There are lots of tools that can let you estimate the size of your potential audience. You can use information from the last census to see how many of your target customers exist in any given area, and you can also find out some interesting things like how many of them have cars, or work in a particular type of industry. This information is available in local libraries as well as online from the Office for National Statistics (www.statistics.gov.uk). Upmystreet.com offers neighbourhood surveys for free, and if you are looking for customers from a particular field of expertise, you can get plenty of information from the relevant trade body.

When I'm considering opening a new health club, I ask an agency called CACI (www.caci.co.uk) to do me a ten-minute drivetime analysis of our new location. They can tell me how many of my target customers live within a ten-minute drive of my target location, and if the figures stack up, then I'll carry on with my research. They charge me a few hundred pounds, but their information stops me wasting thousands. There are hundreds of market research companies out there who can perform similar investigations for you.

Professional market research companies have a whole range of tools that can help you get a clear idea of a) the size of your market, and b) the appetite for your business. It's perfectly possible to replicate some of their tricks yourself. You might not get as accurate results, and they won't impress an investor as much if you include them in your business plan, but at this stage, they will give you a good steer and won't cost you anything.

Start by creating a survey asking people for their thoughts on your business idea and email it to everyone you know. If you don't want them to know it's your business, say you're forwarding it on a friend's behalf, and ask them to forward it to their contacts. Their replies should show you how people feel about your idea. If you get 100 replies and 100 people say they love the idea, then you should be encouraged. If 20 people are positive, then you can look at the other data on the survey – the age, location and income of respondents – to get clues on how best to target those most likely to be your customers.

Of course, you don't have to do this by email. You could put a survey online and ask relevant forum and chat-room users to complete it. Or you could stand in the street with a clipboard and a pen.

You could also try hosting a focus group. You do this by inviting a small group of likely customers to come and discuss their attitudes towards your product or service. There are specialist agencies that charge a lot of money to conduct focus groups for their clients, and there's no way you could replicate the conditions and environment a professional research agency would create, but you could still get some useful information by hosting some focus groups yourself. It is important that whoever chairs the discussion doesn't lead the conversation too much, otherwise the focus group will tend to agree with the chairperson. But if you or someone you know is capable of encouraging people to speak openly, then you might get a very good indication of how the market will respond to your business. There are countless articles online about moderating focus groups, and if you read a couple of them, you'll probably have enough information to have a decent stab at it.

Professional market research agencies have access to all sorts of survey data that is only available to subscribers. They use this data to assess similarities and tendencies in different sections of the population and then employ statisticians to interpret that data. I think it's pretty difficult to replicate all their work on your own, but that doesn't mean you can't employ common sense to get some useful results. Professional researchers will look for comparable businesses and products to see how well they have performed, and you can do this too. You need to identify your nearest types of product or business and investigate how successful (or not) they have been. Scan the trade press, the internet and any other sources you can think of to find out what their sales figures are, what their turnover is and calculate how much of that is likely to be their profit.

The more market research you do at this point, the better position you will be in to assess the opportunity you think you've identified. The one thing I would warn you about is only believing the data you want to believe and ignoring information that's telling you your idea is a dud. The point of your research is to allow you to proceed with confidence, not to pursue your dream at all costs.

How will you find your customers?

It amazes me how many people don't give this enough thought. They just assume that because thousands of babies are born every day they'll have no problem finding customers for their nappy laundry service. There's no point starting a business if you don't know how you'll reach the people who will pay you for your time, expertise, product or service.

For example, if you have identified that your potential customers are upscale professionals in leafy suburbs, how will you let them know you are in business? Advertising is expensive and unless it is extremely well targeted, it can be a waste of money. How else can you reach them? I've read a couple of business books that recommend you think very carefully about finding your first customer and closing your first sale. It's not bad advice, but I think it's better advice to think about where your first 50 customers will come from.

Let me give you some illustrations: I never had problems finding residents for my care homes because local authorities and local hospitals were always looking for places to house patients in need, as were the patients' families. When I open a gym, I can offer discounts on joining fees and membership subscriptions until the club is full, but with the day-care nurseries it was different: even though our facilities were far better than anything else available, parents wouldn't move their child from one nursery to another because the child wouldn't want to be separated from its friends. Instead of opening at full capacity, we had to start offering care for babies, and it was only when they became toddlers that the business grew and we took in more babies: in several nurseries it took us much longer to reach capacity than we'd first thought.

That's why you need to think seriously about where your customers will come from now, because not anticipating barriers to uptake could have a very serious impact on your costs, which in turn will affect your profitability. If you have to spend £100 on marketing to reach a customer who only spends £50 with you, then you're in trouble. If you have to spend £100 reaching a customer who will spend £50 a month with you for the next 12 months, then you're in business.

I talk more about marketing later on in the book, taking you through all sorts of ways of reaching your customers – affiliate deals, PR, piggybacking, advertising – so for now just think generally about how your customers will a) know you exist, and b) spend money with you instead of someone else. If you're going to rely on advertising, then think about where you will advertise and phone up the papers, magazines and websites you want to place adverts in and ask how much they charge. A few phone calls made now may save you from starting something that you won't be able to finish.

● ● ● ● ● BANNATYNE'S BOOTCAMP ● ● ● ● ●

Saving money

I don't pay for flash offices, free lunches for staff, free towels for our health-club members or expensive stationery (my employees laugh because I think they should recycle the paperclips from incoming mail rather than buy a box of new ones). I don't see the sense in spending money unnecessarily, as every pound spent is being deducted from our profits. Having a fancy business card doesn't make you a better entrepreneur, and a bigger office just leads to bigger utility bills. Keeping a tight rein on your expenditure also means you are constantly monitoring your costs, which means you will quickly be alerted to overruns, anomalies and inefficiencies.

● ●

What will you need?

If you're going to be making a product, what supplies will you need? How much will they cost? Who will you buy them from? Will you need staff? If so, how many? What about premises? Will you need to get your products delivered? If so, how much do logistics companies charge?

You need to itemise everything you're going to need to get your product or services in front of your customers, and then you need to put a price on each component. It might help to imagine the sequence of getting from the idea stage to your first sale. Whatever you do, you'll be selling something: in the health-club industry, I need to sell memberships to the public. In the fashion business, designers need to get their clothes into shops. By 'sale' I mean whatever it takes for someone else to give you money in exchange for your time, effort or product.

At Bannatyne Fitness, getting a sale involves knowing the cost of advertising a new club in the relevant local paper, placing that ad just before we're ready to open, maybe doing a leaflet drop for nearby houses, having the staff on site to show prospective members the facilities and for the team at head office to have the time available to process a flood of new applications. Without those things in place, it's going to take me an awful lot longer to get money out of new members.

Don't think about the eventual size of the business and your headquarters in Tokyo, London and New York – just think about everything you'll need to get to that first sale. Make a note of everything you'll have to buy, all the people you'll need to get to know to make it happen and all the talents you'll need to buy in. If you know the price of those items, great; if not, get on the phone and ask suppliers how much they'll charge.

Think logically about everything you will need to produce your product, or start offering your service – for instance, supplies, staff, packaging materials, a banking service that can handle your online payments. And once you've got your list, you need to ask yourself three big questions:

1   How much will it all cost?

2   Do I know where I will get what I need from?

3   Are there any obvious hurdles that I don't know how to get over?

Be honest about your answers, particularly those to question 3. If you do find some hurdles, start talking to people about how you might get over them. Sometimes it can help to break down hurdles into manageable pieces and see them as a series of smaller challenges instead of one big one.

The back-of-the-fag-packet calculation

With every business I've started, I've done a very rough calculation of my costs and revenues to see if there's enough profit in it to make it worth my while. All the analysis you've done until now should enable you to have a pretty good stab at your fag-packet calculation.

At such an early stage, I'm not interested in a detailed breakdown of costs, I just want to sketch out the likely financial shape of the business and see if it will fly. If you're wondering what the Dragons are jotting down in our notebooks while entrepreneurs are pitching to us, we are all doing our own versions of a fag-packet analysis of the opportunity in front of us. If our quick calculation stacks up, then we'll be interested in pursuing the idea further.

You don't need to be able to manage a spreadsheet to do this – pen and paper is fine – but it's much easier to play around with the figures if you can do this electronically. As I've said before, getting up to speed with a basic spreadsheet package should be a priority for a first-time entrepreneur.

To do a fag-packet calculation you need to know the following information:

* How much it costs you to produce your offering

* How much you can charge for it

* How many potential customers you have

The chances are that you will end up doing several versions of your fag-packet calculation, refining it at each stage as more information becomes available. When I started my first care home, I had no idea what certain things would cost me, and when I was working out things like my likely electricity bill, I based it on my home bill. I had six rooms in my house, and if I built a care home with 60 rooms, I just multiplied my bill by ten, and then added on 10 per cent, just in case. Of course, over the next few weeks I did whatever I could to find out the true costs, but that was a good enough figure to start with. Use your common sense: it really doesn't matter at this stage if you don't have precise information to hand.

For your fag-packet calculation, you need to create five columns on your spreadsheet or piece of paper like this:

	Q1	Q2	Q3	Q4	
Average sale price					
Number of customers					
Revenue					
Costs					
Profit					

The Q1 stands for your first quarter in business (i.e. your first three months), the Q2 your second quarter and so on.

In the 'Average sale price' row, write down how much you will charge each customer. On the next row, put in your best guess at the number of customers you will get in your first three months. Now multiply your average sale price by the number of customers to get your total for your 'Revenue' box. Then, next to the 'Costs' heading, tot up everything you need to spend money on in your first three months in business. All you have to do now is deduct your Costs from your Revenue to see what your Profit is. Let me give you an example:

	Q1	Q2	Q3	Q4	
Average sale price	50				
Number of customers	50				
Revenue	2500				
Costs	1500				
Profit	1000				

Of course, you'll have to pay some tax on those profits, but if the figure is enough to get you excited about starting this particular business, you should now sketch out the likely progress in your first year of trading. In this example I'm going to assume a 30 per cent growth in costs and customers for each quarter. In reality, new businesses don't grow at steady rates as they have off-seasons, start-up costs and plenty of other obstacles that can send you off course. When you predict your rate of growth, be realistic about what's achievable: if you are a one-man operation, are you really going to have the capacity to deal with thousands of customers?

	Q1	Q2	Q3	Q4
Average sale price	50	50	50	50
Numbers of customers	50	65	84.5	100
Revenue	2500	3250	4225	5492
Costs	1500	1950	2535	3295
Profits	1000	1300	1690	2197

If this were a real business, I have to say, I wouldn't be very interested in it. Making a profit of £1000 a month isn't a big enough return for all the effort it takes to get a new business off the ground. However, if you can start this business by doing a bit of moonlighting in your spare time and use your first year in business to build up credibility and confidence, then maybe a calculation like this will give you the confidence to get started.

The point I'm making is that you've got to like the sort of business you're creating. Getting a business off the ground takes unbelievable amounts of hard work, so you've got to love what you do. On those days when you feel like giving up, you've got to be motivated by your dream of what the business will become. If the outcome of your fag-packet analysis isn't lighting a fire somewhere inside you, then you've got two things to consider: a) ditching the idea, or b) making it better.

It isn't difficult to work out how you can make a business better, it just requires a careful evaluation of all your assumptions – how many customers can you get, how much can you charge, what costs can you keep to an absolute minimum, what additional products or services can you supply, how quickly can you expand?

Sensitivity analysis

Once you're happy with your fag-packet calculation, you ought to do what accountants call a 'sensitivity analysis'. This means finding out how sensitive your fledgling business is to error. For instance, what happens if you've underestimated your costs and they are 30 per cent higher than you expected? Can you still make money? And will you still be in profit if your sales are 10 per cent lower than you predicted?

Adjust each of your assumptions in increments of 10 per cent and see how close you are to losing money. If you fail to break even – or earn enough to live on – when your figures dip by 10 or 20 per cent, then I'd advise you to think of another business idea. Personally, I like to know my sales can drop 40 per cent and my costs can go up by a similar amount before I go into the red.

In a separate analysis, you should also see what happens to your cashflow if interest rates go up by a couple of per cent. If you have a large loan, even a small rate rise makes a difference to your outgoings as the chart below shows.

Monthly repayments on a £50,000 loan repaid over 10 years:

5%	6%	7%	8%	9%	10%	11%	12%
£530	£555	£581	£607	£633	£661	£689	£717

Source: FSA's loan calculator

A lot has been written about the need for entrepreneurs to take risks. There's absolutely no doubt that starting a business is a risk, but it is a *calculated* risk, and your sensitivity analysis is what lets you calculate the size of that risk.

Top ten reasons why some new businesses fail

1 **The founders don't do enough research.** In my view, this probably accounts for most business failures.

2 **The founders aren't honest with themselves.** They either overestimate their abilities or, more often, the size of their customer base and the amount customers will be prepared to pay.

3 **The founders move too quickly.** They get so caught up in their idea that they don't build a solid financial basis for their enterprise.

4 **The founders move too slowly.** Ideas are ten a penny, and if you don't move on an opportunity when you spot one, there's a very good chance someone else will have the same idea and take your potential customer base away from you.

5 **The founders get their supply and demand levels out of kilter.** Either they have too much stock or not enough; too many staff or not enough.

6 **The founders don't understand cashflow.** Calculating profit and loss and cashflow aren't the same thing. If you run out of cash, you run out of time.

7 **The founders spend too much money.** This is usually on things that don't help the business, such as flash cars and offices. If you spend it before you've made it, you'll end up bankrupt.

8 **The founders give up.** When things get tough, some people just can't face fighting any harder and they walk away. They let one bad week convince them they will only ever have bad weeks and they throw in the towel. Every new business hits crisis points, and that's when you have to dig a little deeper and work a little harder.

9 **The founders didn't do their sensitivity analysis.** If your costs go up, or you need to drop your prices to remain competitive, how quickly

would you end up in the red? If your margins are too narrow, look again at your business model and see if you can make it more robust. When you're starting a business you can't be sure that your predictions are accurate, so it's wise to build a wide margin of error into your initial calculations.

10 **The founders didn't work hard enough.** Either they employed people to do work they were capable of doing themselves, or they shirked from picking up the phone and making a sale, or they skived when they should have been getting stuck in.

You'll have noticed that the reasons why businesses fail are all to do with the founders, not market conditions, recessions, suppliers going bust or any other excuse you can think of. If your supplier goes bust, you need to take responsibility for using the wrong supplier.

> ❛ *There's absolutely no doubt that starting a business is a risk, but it is a* calculated *risk, and your sensitivity analysis is what lets you calculate the size of that risk.* ❜

SWOT analysis

This is one of the oldest pieces of management jargon and unlike others that have come and gone, this one still gets mentioned because it remains a crucial tool for assessing any business opportunity.

SWOT stands for Strengths, Weaknesses, Opportunities and Threats, and by looking at each of these categories, you build up a picture of how your business fits into the surrounding context. It's all very well imagining a perfect business selling the best sandwiches in the world, but what if someone opens for business down the road selling sandwiches that are only marginally less tasty than yours? The biggest plus of a SWOT analysis is that it forces you to get some perspective on your idea. So, taking each category in turn, what sort of things should go into your SWOT analysis?

Strengths

What do you do better than anyone else? Is your product, service, location or price better than the competition? Are you the first person to offer this to the market? Is there a genuine need for your offering? Think critically about the reasons why you believe there's a business in your idea and list everything that gives you an advantage.

Weaknesses

This section is about identifying your vulnerabilities. Are you exposed to someone pinching your idea or your customers? If so, how do you defend yourself? Do you need to consider patents or trademarks? Are your prices too high? Is your service untried? How able are you to cope with changes to your market? For instance, if you want to open a hotel, what happens if the weather is terrible and tourists don't want to visit? Are you (and the fact you're inexperienced) the weakness? How easy will it be to recruit staff, and hold on to them? Similarly, how easy will it be to reach your customers and get them to keep coming back?

Opportunities

This is where you look around you, and to the future, to see where your best chances of finding new customers are, or how you might be able to charge them more or get a better deal from your suppliers. Is there an event coming up that you can make use of? Is there a demographic shift – like an ageing population – that you will benefit from?

Threats

The obvious thing to list here is who your rivals are. Now ask yourself how they might respond to your launch. Will they drop their prices, increase their marketing or poach your staff? Just as with the Opportunities, look to the future and see if you can anticipate where the danger lies. Is it possible that technological advances will mean your customers can easily do for themselves what you're proposing to do for them? Are there environmental factors that could impact on your idea? Or political changes? What if the planning laws change, taxes rise, interest rates go up or there's a crash in the property market? How would your business cope in these situations?

In the early days of a business, I think you should be doing a new SWOT analysis every quarter. As you make contacts, do your research and get feedback from your first customers, you will find things out about your business, your market and your rivals that could change the course your business needs to take. As the business matures, carry on doing them every six months.

This may sound obvious, but you should always be looking at ways to maximise and defend your Strengths while minimising your Weaknesses and finding ways to compensate for them. You should also constantly look for new Opportunities and new Threats, and keep reviewing how you will respond to them.

I still do SWOT analyses for my health clubs. When we realised that one of our strengths was some spare land next to our Durham club, we saw the opportunity to build a hotel on it where guests could make use of the club's facilities. When we did a SWOT analysis after acquiring a chain of clubs from Hilton hotels, we discovered that we had several locations where we had a health club, a hotel and a spa all together. We realised that this gave us the opportunity to market 'spa weekend packages'.

Interestingly, one business's strength can be another's weakness. I bet if David Lloyd Leisure did a SWOT analysis, one of their strengths would be the fact that they have so many tennis courts. They offer kids tennis clubs, and are arguably the market leaders in tennis. But one of Bannatyne Fitness's strengths is that we *don't* do tennis: we don't fill our clubs with kids, and we can build on much smaller plots, which means our costs are lower.

When you look at your SWOT analysis, try seeing if someone else could make a business out of your weaknesses – not only will it help you define your offering, but it will force you to view your business from a different angle.

Defending your idea

If you have developed a new product or have an innovative new service, you need to think about how you can protect yourself from a copycat rival. I've learnt that ideas are cheap and that execution and delivery are the best ways to defend your business, but if you have a genuinely new product, then you should spend some time looking into how you can legally protect it.

The Intellectual Property Office (www.ipo.gov.uk) can take you through the process (and costs) of registering your product for patent protection. There are specialist patent lawyers, but if you use them, you will only be paying for something you can easily do yourself. However, be prepared to find out that your invention is unpatentable, or at least not patentable in the way you anticipate.

You cannot patent an idea, only a piece of working technology that is sufficiently different from existing patented technology. Even then, there is nothing to stop a rival from looking at your product and figuring out how to produce a similar piece of kit using different processes, thereby avoiding infringing your patent. You should be prepared for the Intellectual Property Office to refuse a patent because your idea is too similar to an existing one.

I have occasionally been approached by entrepreneurs seeking investment for a product so cutting edge, so innovative and so revolutionary that they won't tell me what it is! I understand that inventors feel nervous about people stealing their idea, but the truth is that most people are lazy, sceptical and too busy with their own lives to get out of their ruts and steal your thunder. It can happen, but in my experience, you have much more to gain by sharing your idea with people who can help you refine it and make a profit from it. Be a bit careful, but let yourself be guided by common sense, not paranoia.

The Intellectual Property Office also offers advice on other ways in which you can defend your idea, including trademarking. This prevents a rival from using your company name, product name or branding to pass off their copycat product as yours. Trademarking is a complex area, and you need to apply for separate trademarks for all the areas you trade in, for instance in retail *and* online, and they charge for each sector. It can be an expensive outlay for a new business, but you can always expand the areas your trademark applies to later on.

In a few special cases, you can give yourself protection by lodging your business plan with a solicitor. A high-profile case in the past few years was brought by Simon Fuller, who devised the *Pop Idol* TV format, against Simon Cowell, who developed *The X Factor*. Simon Fuller didn't own the idea of TV talent shows, but so much of *The X Factor* was similar to *Pop Idol* – down to the sets and the production crew – that Simon Cowell now pays a share of his *X Factor* profits to Simon Fuller. If you can write a 'bible' of how your business operates and what makes it special, a lawyer may be able to advise you if this protects someone from replicating your business so precisely that they have infringed your intellectual property rights.

Is it the right idea for you?

This is a very basic question, but the answer is absolutely crucial. The best businesses are started when the founder's skills fit the opportunity. Does the business you're imagining feel like a business you could run? Does it feel like a business you could be proud of? Just because you enjoy drinking beer, it doesn't necessarily mean you'll enjoy selling it.

You don't have to have all the skills, or all the contacts; you just need to feel confident that you can acquire the skills (or hire them, or buy them in) and confident that you can assemble everything you need to build the company you're imagining.

Ask yourself if you like what you're imagining. I can't say often enough how hard you are going to have to work to make a success of any new business, so if you don't like it, you're not going to enjoy it. What kind of business do you want to be in charge of? Do you want a local business serving local customers with limited scope for expansion? Do you want to own a national or international brand? Do you want to sell it for millions in ten years' time? Or do you want something that allows you to pick the kids up from school? Now ask yourself if the business you're developing in your mind is capable of being the business of your dreams.

I truly believe that the best businesses aren't always the biggest businesses. A good business, in my view, is one that makes its owners happy, one that gives them a good quality of life, that fits in with their lifestyle and makes them proud. I used to work as a mechanic and briefly ran my own garage when I lived on Jersey in my twenties. Even though I'd spent a couple of grand on equipment, I walked away from it because I realised I hated being covered in oil and working under a bonnet when I could have been selling ice creams on the beach and talking to girls! Please don't think I'm suggesting you should abandon an idea just because it's not a £1 million idea. If it's capable of being the business you want, then it's worth a lot more than money to you.

One of the reasons why I got out of the ice-cream business and into care homes was because my daughters were growing up. I no longer wanted to run a business that meant I was working after school and at weekends when I wanted to be with them. With the care homes, I knew I could employ a manager and not have to work such long hours. And a few years later when I opened my first health club, I liked the idea of running a business that didn't operate 24 hours a day – those panicked phone calls in the middle of the night were something I wanted to eliminate from my life. This is the sort of thing I think you should consider when you decide if your idea is the right business for you.

And if it's not the right business for you?

Taking part in *Dragons' Den* for nearly five years has given me the opportunity to see all sorts of fledgling businesses that I would never otherwise be aware of, usually because they would have failed before they reached the public's attention. It's notable how often one of the Dragons tells an entrepreneur that they don't have a business, but that they do have a product or an idea that they should take to an existing company.

People come up with all sorts of innovations that modify or improve existing businesses or products, and more often than not they would be better off taking their idea directly to the companies they think they can compete against. Let's just say that you have an idea to make bicycles safer. What's the point in taking on Dawes, Cannondale and Ridgeback when you could go to one of the big firms and tell them you know a way they can beat the competition? If they're smart, they'll pay you for your idea.

I've heard the following story so many times that it makes me wonder if it can be true. It doesn't really matter either way, though, because it contains a truth about business, and that's what I want to get across. One day a man had an idea about how he could make a box of matches more cheaply than any of the existing matchmakers. However, he realised he couldn't take on the established players, so he made an appointment to see the managing director of Swan Vesta. He said, 'I know a way your company could save a million pounds every year.' Naturally, the MD was interested, so they discussed a deal and drew up the necessary legal paperwork. Then the man revealed his big idea: 'If you only put a phosphorus strip on one side of the box, it wouldn't harm your sales, and you would halve the amount of phosphorus you need.' If the story's true, this man was smart enough to know that he had an idea for a business but that there wasn't a business in the idea. However, it didn't stop him making money from it.

> **'** *Just because you've got an idea for a business, it doesn't necessarily mean there's a business in the idea.* **'**

Idea checklist

* Are you passionate about your idea? It's going to dominate your life for the next few years, so ask yourself if you love it enough to let it take over.

* Can it make money? Are you convinced that it can provide you with a decent income?

* Is your idea capable of being turned into a business that will satisfy your dreams? Basically, you need to ask yourself if it will make you happy.

* How does it make you feel when you think about it? If it's the right idea, it will get your brain thinking twenty things at once, your blood pumping and a slight smile should creep across your face!

The biggest myths about starting a business

The Department for Business, Enterprise and Regulatory Reform (BERR) carried out some research into why so many people talk about starting a business but never actually get round to it. They discovered that there are seven widely believed myths about becoming an entrepreneur that put people off.

It seems the biggest factors pushing would-be entrepreneurs away from starting up are fears about raising finance, the time it takes to run a business and the volume and complexity of red tape they anticipate.

Myth No. 1: Around the same number of entrepreneurs buy an existing business as start from scratch.
In actual fact, nearly three-quarters of businesses are started from scratch, far higher than survey respondents thought. Respondents said they felt it was harder to start a new business than is actually the case, which is how we get our second myth…

Myth No. 2: It takes years to start a business from scratch.
Research shows that most businesses are established within six months. Those people thinking about – or avoiding starting a business – assume it takes substantially longer, and this puts them off.

Myth No. 3: It's hard to get a bank loan to start a business.
While I know it's harder to get a loan if you haven't got a track record, statistics show that only 10–20 per cent of applications for business loans are rejected. Respondents thought the figure was much higher. The survey did find that those in what they called 'lower socio-economic groups' and who lacked any collateral accounted for most of the rejections.

Myth No. 4: A business plan is essential to starting a business.
There's little doubt a business plan is useful, but it certainly isn't necessary. Established operators downplayed the importance of a business plan, although they did say that the learning process that accompanies the writing of a business plan can be more important than the plan itself. If you really can't face writing a business plan, it doesn't mean you can't start a business.

Myth No. 5: Small businesses don't generate much turnover in their first year.
This figure is fascinating: average income, forecast by first-time entrepreneurs for their first year of trading, is generally only half of the figure

actually achieved by small businesses. A lot of people believe that it would be difficult to make an adequate living from a small firm – and that's just not the case.

Myth No. 6: Small firms spend all their time dealing with red tape. Business owners who took part in the research estimated that they spent around five hours per week dealing with bureaucracy, while non-entrepreneurs thought the red-tape burden would be nearly twice as large. Don't let these mythical extra hours of paperwork put you off.

Myth No. 7: Most small firms fail within the first year.
In fact, the opposite is true: 80–90 per cent of small firms are still trading 12 months after start-up. This myth is widespread and it inflates the degree of risk felt by those thinking of starting their own business.

There was an eighth myth the research uncovered, and that's a misguided belief that there are tax advantages to self-employment. This has the effect of encouraging people to start a business because they think their tax burden will be lower. You can offset certain expenses, but you still have to pay your taxes!

IIIIIIIIIIIIIIIIIIIIIIIIIIIIIIIIII **CASE STUDY** IIIIIIIIIIIIIIIIIIIIIIIIIIIIIIIII

Name: Anthony Coates-Smith **Age**: 31
Job: MD, Igloo Thermo-Logistics Ltd
Qualifications: Degree in accountancy and economics
www.igloo-thermo.com

Igloo operates a temperature-controlled delivery network, primarily serving the catering and pharmaceutical industries. I started the business in 2004 with my partner, Alistair Turner, after the company we worked for – Brake Bros, which delivers food to the catering trade – continually experienced difficulties finding reliable temperature-controlled delivery companies. Our former employer is now one of our biggest clients.

The thermo-logistics industry was very fragmented in the UK, and there was no single company that Brake Bros could turn to for their chilled deliveries. We might find someone good in one town, but in another the guy wouldn't turn up to work if there was an England match on TV! Alistair and I thought that if a 'white-van man' could make a living out of refrigerated transport without the knowledge Alistair and I had from working in the industry, and without the economies of scale of a larger organisation, then we stood a very good chance. If we could offer good customer service and good communication with our clients, then we knew we would be able to take business away from other operators.

We talked about it for a couple of months until one Monday morning we discovered that Brake Bros had paid £13,000 in one weekend on external delivery companies – we knew then that we couldn't just make a living but that there was a real opportunity to build a very big business. That was in November, and we spent until the following April when we resigned doing our research.

The first thing we did was read books by other entrepreneurs to get their insights and advice on starting a business. Then we Googled 'business-plan template' and discovered one on HSBC's website that we worked through. We found writing a business plan very helpful and actually prepared three different versions – one if we made mistakes and our fleet was under-utilised, the other if we had fairly mediocre success and the third if we were fully utilised. I think that made us look at our business from three different per-spectives and made us very flexible. Sometimes entrepreneurs can only see one vision for their future, and I don't think that helps if things don't go to plan.

Right from the start, we decided that we didn't want to take a drop in salary, so we started our calculations from there: if we needed to earn X, then we needed to do so many deliveries a week, which we calculated meant operating a fleet of four vans to start with, quickly growing to six by the end of our first year. Our backgrounds as supply chain managers, and our degrees, definitely helped us in our planning and we used Gantt charts (that help you plan tasks in the right order) and Prince software for our project management templates. We then costed buying the vans and paying the staff, and once we had factored in everything, we predicted we needed £100,000 to start the business.

We were shocked to find out how risk-averse the banks were and we had to offer our homes as security against the loan. This meant involv-ing our partners, as we wanted them both to know what starting a business would take. We made the decision that we would rather take the risk at 27 than later in life when we might have additional respon-sibilities and larger families. It was now or never.

We rented space from Regus Offices so that we didn't have to worry about paying the rates or our IT support, and I remember very clearly sitting there nervously in our first week, with four gleaming vans outside, waiting for the phone to ring. After a week, we took our first order from a supplier I'd known at Brakes. They then recommended us to their contacts, and things started to take off.

Our budget in the first year meant that Alistair and I drove two of the vans so we only had to pay for two additional drivers. When all four vans were out on deliveries, phone calls were diverted to our mobiles and we'd take orders on the road. Then we had a stroke of luck when Brake Bros phoned and booked up all four vans for three months solidly.

Not only did our previous careers give us a few useful contacts, but it also gave us the knowledge that many clients would take months to pay their bills – it's just the way the industry works. So from the very start we allowed for what's known as a 'factoring' charge. This meant that as soon as we raised an invoice, our bank credited 85 per cent of that invoice to our account. When the invoice was finally paid, the bank kept 3 per cent of the money and forwarded the other 12 per cent to us. Obviously, this is a big expense, but if we hadn't made allowances for it, our cashflow would have been terrible.

No one believes us, but in those first 18 months we both worked a minimum of 100 hours a week. When the manager at Regus found Alistair in the office one morning with a towel round his waist and a toothbrush in his mouth, we were issued with an eviction notice – just the day before, she'd found me asleep on the sofa! In the end it worked in our favour, as it prompted us to get more suitable premises and our first depot.

In the early days, Alistair and I did everything ourselves – marketing, sales and admin as well as half the driving – and I was so exhausted that I actually started to have blackouts. We were spending far more time with each other than we were with our partners, but we were always there to support each other. There's not much I would do differently, but I do wish we had taken the decision to stop driving the vans ourselves earlier. It was a tough decision as it meant turning customers away when there was an empty van parked outside, and for a couple of months that decision cost us money. However, it freed us up to think strategically, and after three months, our sales chart went vertical and it's pretty much been the same ever since.

We started to keep a list of all the customers we were having to turn down because we were so busy. We realised there was a chance that if one of our rivals did a good job, we may never get those customers back, so we decided to expand more rapidly. To do that we needed additional funds. Despite our track record, the banks still wanted our homes as security, so we decided to look at other forms of investment. We were big fans of *Dragons' Den* and had watched it in the office when we were working late. We were often amazed at some of the poor businesses entrepreneurs were taking into the Den, and we thought we could offer the Dragons a real chance to make money. Even if we didn't get backing, we were pretty sure we would get some very valuable PR out of it.

We appeared in Series 3 of *Dragons' Den* in 2006 and we were in there for 90 minutes. We came out with Duncan Bannatyne and Richard Farleigh as our new shareholders: they took 22.5 per cent of the equity between them for an investment of £160,000.

It's great to have two such experienced investors at the end of the phone and their investment has enabled us to buy more vans and expand our service. They want to know if we have a problem and they want to share our successes, but other than that they leave us alone to grow the business. Their investment has allowed us to expand rapidly and we are now turning over £3 million a year and looking to double that each year for the next few years.

What's the best advice you've ever had? Alistair's dad said something very important to us and that was, 'Don't hide behind your desks.' It's too easy, he said, to send emails and build websites, but the best way to grow a business and to keep your customers is to meet them, to look them in the eye and to listen to them. He was right.

What do you wish you'd known from the start? I wish we'd made the decision to stop driving the vans earlier.

What's the one thing you'd say to someone starting their first business? Get a good accountant, don't scrimp on a bad one, and when you get your figures, study them, scrutinise them and constantly review them. If you don't know your figures, you don't know your business.

||||||||||||||||||||||||||||||||||||||||||||||||||||||||||||||||||||||||||||||||||||||

3 You

The single biggest reason why some new businesses fail is because the founder made mistakes. In my opinion, the founders are the most important part of every new business and this chapter is all about getting you into entrepreneurial shape.

Whether you're starting a multinational operation, a social venture or a corner shop, you need to know what you're capable of. You might be starting out on your own or as part of a team, but either way, you are going to be working like crazy to get your business off the ground, and at times you are going to get frustrated, distracted and despondent. Knowing how you'll respond in certain situations and knowing where your strengths and weaknesses lie will help you reach for the right kind of help and give you a greater chance of success. I've found a couple of tests that can help you discover what you're good at, but before we get on to those, I want to talk about the two most important qualities an entrepreneur needs. I haven't worked out a way to teach these, so I'm just going to tell it to you straight. I don't have many rules, but these two are absolutely non-negotiable.

Rule 1 – Take responsibility for your company

Whether you're in business on your own or in a partnership or part of a founding team, the success of your venture will come down to you. Accepting this single fact is, I believe, the most important lesson a new entrepreneur needs to learn.

When I say 'company', it doesn't matter at this point if you're not much beyond the idea phase. I'm certainly not just referring to limited companies, plcs or businesses with a particular trading status – we'll come to those practicalities much later in this book – I mean the venture that you're in charge of, at whatever stage of development it's at.

Have you ever noticed that when companies explain poor performance they say things like 'Sales are down this quarter because we've had very bad weather' or 'Our suppliers let us down' or 'We had a lot of competition from China.' The real reason they performed poorly was because their chief executive hadn't planned for the possibility of bad weather or unreliable suppliers or wasn't able to respond quickly enough to a new competitor from overseas.

Similarly, if your business fails, it will be because you failed. Maybe you didn't do your research, didn't hire the right staff, didn't listen to advice or spent too much money on the wrong things. A willingness to take responsibility for your actions and those of your company is the most important attribute an entrepreneur must possess. Stop making excuses and start finding solutions.

Rule 2 – Work hard

These days, I spend about five hours a week in the office. I have successfully delegated to a brilliant team who run my businesses for me so I can write books and make TV shows. But it wasn't always like that. Whenever I have started a business, it has consumed my life and I have worked 18-hour days, sometimes for 60 days at a stretch without a break. Getting a business off the ground requires a phenomenal amount of effort, as not only do you need to do whatever it is that makes your company money – manufacture a product, perform a service, or import and export – you also need to take care of the admin side of things, possibly raise finance, hire staff, find premises, network to make the contacts that might transform your business, etc. To start with, you could be doing the work of three or more people. Possibly even three teams of people.

The good news is that you'll be learning new skills and meeting new people all the time, and this is invariably exciting and stimulating. Starting a business can be so much fun that you can't really call it work. It's more of a passion. Or maybe even a drug. However, when you work that hard, you can forget to do things like eat and sleep. You might be excited about an upcoming meeting, or worried about it, and burning all that nervous energy can take its toll. You can be susceptible to bugs you would have fought off if you were taking proper care of yourself, and you'll have no choice but to work through bouts of minor illnesses.

When you put your head above the parapet and have hundreds of meetings with customers, investors and suppliers, you leave yourself open to levels of criticism you probably haven't experienced before. If you make 100 calls, the chances are you'll get 90 rejections, and everyone finds that demoralising. It can be easy to give up. It's even easier to give yourself the afternoon off, but when you do this, doubts start to creep in and you lose momentum. When you're already on the move, it's much easier to keep going forward than it is if you stop and start. New businesses need to be powered through by their founders, and even though it can be like carrying a huge weight up a mountain, you just have to keep going.

There will also be times when friends call you up and say you've been missed at the pub/rugby team/committee meeting, and they'll try to twist your arm and persuade you to leave your business for a few hours and let your hair down. Only you can decide if you'd rather have a pint or give your new business everything you have.

You might also have to make the tough decision not to go to a friend's wedding, or a child's school play, or even let the family go on holiday without you. It won't be for ever, though, so just tell them that when you've made your fortune, you'll be able to work a five-hour week and you'll have plenty of time – and money – to make it up to them. In the meantime, though, you don't have any choice but to get your head down and keep on working.

The ideal entrepreneur

I believe the best entrepreneurs share many of the same qualities. I'd like to run through the skills and attributes that indicate success in business and show how many of these can be learnt by anybody.

Not every entrepreneur possesses all of these, but most of the successful ones will have four out of five of these traits. In fact, if you recognise yourself in each of these categories, then you probably have the makings of the best entrepreneur in the world! Often new businesses have a handful of founders, and the most successful launch teams are those where each member possesses one of these complementary key attributes. If you don't see much of yourself in these categories, then make a note of where you fall short, and use the advice here to bolster your weak areas.

1 The ability to focus

An entrepreneur who is launching a new business doesn't have a typical day. You can go from negotiating with suppliers to hiring staff to finding premises to raising finance to selling your wares to dealing with complaints – all within an hour. It's exhilarating and challenging, but it's also dangerous.

It's very easy to get caught up in the momentum a new business somehow creates. It can start carrying you along, rather than you guiding it. It's easy for small and agile new businesses to change direction, jump on bandwagons and respond to new ideas. This is great – it's a major commercial advantage to be flexible and responsive – but it's also possible that a few months down the line your business will have become something different, less focused and less effective.

If you're leading a team, the people around you look to you to make decisions, and if you've never been in this position before, it can be nerve-wracking. Employees, customers and clients expect you to know what's best for your company, and you need to come up with answers.

How to focus

As it's so easy to get distracted, you might find it helps to take a moment now to make a note of what your company is about. Take a sheet of paper – it could be in your diary, it could be on a Post-It note, it could be on a giant sheet of A1 that you're going to pin to the wall – and write down the following:

A. What does your business do?

By this I mean what is its primary aim. You might make widgets and wotsits and thingummies, but that's an activity, not a business. Your business is in making the *best* widgets and wotsits, or making the *cheapest* thingummies, or being the *only* company that supplies all three. Take a moment to work out exactly why you're starting this business, and write it down as succinctly as you can.

B. What excites you about the business?

When it gets tough, you need to remind yourself of what inspired you in the first place. What is it about this business that makes you get out of bed in the morning and work like a slave?

C. What do you want out of it?

Are you in it just for the money? Do you want to be the biggest, or the best? Do you want to make your company a household name? Whatever it is, write it down.

Now put that bit of paper in your top drawer or pin it up above your desk. Look at it regularly and make sure that everything you do, every decision you make, helps you to focus on these three things. Don't let a new opportunity drag you down a new road unless it brings you closer to satisfying these criteria you've set down for yourself. As long as you are moving towards your goal, you have the flexibility to duck and dive and try things out. So long as you remind yourself of these ambitions on a weekly basis, you shouldn't lose focus for long.

2 The ability to sell

Whatever you do to make money, you need to be able to sell your product to customers, yourself to investors and even your dream to your employees. We all have to sell something, and those of us who can do it well tend to earn a lot more money than those who can't.

Selling makes most people nervous. They envisage cold-calling people out of the phone book and getting the phone slammed down on them. Selling should never be like that. At its best, selling makes everyone's lives better because people find out about products and services that they want or need. Good salespeople make other people happy.

If you're really worried about having to make sales to get your company off the ground, then you would do well to buy a specialist book on sales, or even go for some coaching. It will be money well spent. I'm not a salesman, but I have learnt enough about the basic mechanics of salesmanship to allow me to sell myself and my businesses effectively. What follows is a crash course in how to become better at selling.

How to sell

Firstly...make sure you're talking to the right people. The reason why cold-calling doesn't work is that most people won't want what you're selling. You need to identify the people who will need and benefit from your offering. Think about how you can reach your likeliest customers. And when you've identified them, make sure you speak to someone who can say 'yes'. If you want a company or individual to place an order with you, you need to know that the person you're speaking to can authorise the purchase. You wouldn't try to sell a car to a five-year-old: you need to speak to the parent. Targeting your sales to the right people can save you an awful lot of time.

Secondly...if you can make life better for the person you're selling to, you should feel good about making contact with them, not apologetic. If you need a loan from the bank, the best way to do that is to convince the bank manager that you will make the bank money. Focus on what's in it for them: can you save them time, money, hassle? Can you make them feel better about themselves? By understanding what they get out of the transaction, you are far more likely to get what you want out of it.

Thirdly...you have to close the sale. You need to give people a reason to choose you *now*. Work out deals that give people an incentive to say yes. When I open a new health club, we'll usually have an introductory offer whereby the first 100 members won't have to pay the joining fee. The next 100 will get a 90 per cent reduction on the joining fee, and so on until we're full. If we didn't offer these incentives, it would take us a lot longer to reach capacity as members would take their time to decide to join. What can you do to make people say yes immediately? A time-limited offer? An introductory rate? A faster turnaround?

Finally...expect rejection. Some salesmen tell me they have to make ten phone calls to get a sale, others say the figure is closer to 100. People will have all sorts of reasons why they don't want to change suppliers, add to their monthly outgoings or make a new purchase, and the best salespeople are those who find as many possible ways of overcoming the objections of their potential customers. The more you get to know your customers, the more you'll be able to respond to their questions, and the levels of rejection you experience will drop. Nevertheless, even the very best sales professionals get doors slammed in their faces – it's part of the job.

The key thing I want you to grasp is that selling isn't frightening, or even particularly difficult. Approached in the right way, it can be fun. If you can't sell your business, then it will come across that you don't believe in your business, so you have to overcome your reservations. All you have to do is find someone whose life will be better if they had what you're selling: think of it as helping, not selling.

3 The ability to inspire

I want you to think for a moment about how other people see you and your business. Imagine you want someone to invest in you, or lend you money, or come and work for you. What do you think those people need to see before they take the plunge?

Speaking generally, employees and clients want to be inspired. They need to know enough of your vision to be able to share it. They need to understand why you're giving up everything to start this business. They want to be sure that you will be giving it 110 per cent every single day.

Inspiring people isn't just about selling yourself to them, it's about making them as confident about your business as you are. If you are rock sure about your offering, your figures and your projections, this will come a lot easier. You might have heard investors say that they didn't invest in the idea, they invested in the person, and whether you're asking people for their cash or their time, one way or another they are ultimately investing in you.

The most inspirational people I know aren't always the best sales people (although there's no doubt that helps), they are the people who I believe in. Whether it's the nerdy inventor who makes a hash of his presentation on *Dragons' Den*, or Gordon Ramsay, the reason why I back them for success is because I can see how passionate they are about their business. Lord knows I'm not the best salesman, or the slickest operator – and in my early days in business I was far from polished – but no one doubted that I believed in myself and I was passionate about my business, and this helped me build a team and a company. I don't stand in front of my staff all the time and give them sermons on how they can achieve great things, nor do you have to have the charisma of a rock star to do it, it's much less obvious than that. So, how do you inspire people?

How to be inspirational

A. Know your business inside out.
Know what the cashflow will be in Month 5, know which markets you'll target in Year 2, know the name of the person who empties the bins in your office. The more you know, the more you can lead, and the more you'll inspire people.

B. Be positive.
Focus on the upside and tell everyone you meet about the benefits of your venture. Listen to other people, especially when they have something critical to say about your business, as this shows you are sensitive and adaptable, rather than pig-headed and bloody-minded. But above all else, smile.

C. Show your desire.
If I believe you want it enough to work hard for it, I'm more likely to want to tag along for the ride.

4 The ability to manage
Whether it's people, resources or data, a successful entrepreneur needs to be organised. Data needs to be stored so it can be easily and fruitfully accessed, and people need to be properly trained and incentivised.

How to manage data
There are certain management tools you can implement that make managing data a lot easier, most of which involve using a computer. You also need to keep paper records of certain transactions.

* Use the software that came bundled with your computer to create a database of contacts, customers and anyone else who might be valuable to your organisation.

* Use a spreadsheet to keep on top of your expenditure and income.

* Stock up on lever-arch files and keep all your receipts and invoices in date order.

* Get a big page-to-a-day diary and write in all your appointments and reminders to follow up on calls and meetings. Or use the diary on your BlackBerry or iCal and set up alerts so you never miss a meeting.

The secret to data management is 'little and often'. It can actually be therapeutic to end the day, or the week, with an hour doing your accounts and paperwork. If you let it build up, not only are you storing up a big headache for yourself down the line, but you are forfeiting the opportunity to understand your business better. The closer you are to your data, the more you can identify trends in transaction levels, the more likely you are to spot a discrepancy, and the more you will understand your business. Even the smallest businesses benefit from filing everything in an orderly fashion.

How to manage people

Managing people requires different tools. If you're part of a management team, you want to make sure that everyone's roles are well defined and that you each know what you are responsible for, so that you don't step on each other's toes. These are my guidelines for effective people management:

* Agree what each of you is responsible for.

* Set an achievable target (x sales, y gizmos produced, z pounds saved from the budget) for each of you.

* Set a deadline for achieving those targets.

* Meet at a regular time and place to update each other on your progress.

Aside from that, leave each person to get on with his or her own job. When you're excited about something, it's easy to do a whole lot of talking and forget to do the work. When you're all hyped about your venture, there's a natural tendency to want to get involved in everything, and that leads to meddling, a duplication of tasks, time-wasting and conflict. The people who work for you need to know what is expected of them, how their work will be monitored, what they have the authority to do without referring to you and the timeframes they are expected to work to. No one appreciates a boss – or a business partner – who micro-manages their every move, and once the boundaries have been set, you should stick to them.

It can be very difficult for an entrepreneur to delegate activities that are key to the success of their company. But if you have the right team, and are structuring their work effectively, then by letting them get on with their job, it frees you up to build and strengthen the company. A successful entrepreneur is one who can delegate effectively.

I have always found delegation natural. For me it's just common sense: after all, I can't be in two places at once or do everything myself. However, I know some people really struggle to set their staff free to do their jobs properly. If you're finding it hard, I think you need to ask yourself a question: *is the problem with you or your team?* Delegation is easier if you are delegating to good people; if you have the wrong people, then it's no wonder you're reluctant to let go. Maybe you need to train your staff more, motivate them more effectively, or maybe you need to hire more able employees. If it's you that's the problem, then I suggest you take it in stages. Give someone a small project to do, assess how they perform and take it from there. A good way to do this is simply to take a day off. Leave someone else in charge for a day and see how they respond. Build up trust with your team in stages: give them a chance to ease your doubts, and delegation will become a natural part of your management style.

> ❝ *A successful entrepreneur is one who can delegate effectively.* ❞

5 The ability to see things through

Do you want to know what the difference is between successful and unsuccessful entrepreneurs? Ultimately, it's very simple: it comes down to perseverance. Almost every venture I've ever been involved in or been witness to could have gone belly up at some point in the early days. In fact, there was probably a point when a sane person would have thrown in the towel.

Successful entrepreneurs have so much belief in their business that they can ignore what often seems like common sense. Their belief and their passion mean they'll take a loan on a high-interest credit card to get through the crunch months, or they'll advertise for customers before they've got the product in place, or any number of other risky activities that most people baulk at.

When I opened my first care home in 1986, I found it impossible to get backing from the banks. I got turned down by every lender, but I knew that the business I wanted to start was a good one. So I sold every asset I had to get the money together for building to start. Then every six weeks I had to pay the builders another instalment: I remortgaged properties I owned; I sold others and used cashflow from the ice-cream business to meet their bills. By the end of construction I had sold my house and taken £30,000 out on credit cards: I would have done whatever it took to get that nursing home built and open for business. It was painful, but it was absolutely worth it.

When you get demoralised, when you get rejected, when 15 different people want 20 different things from you by 2 p.m., you'd have to be an alien not to want to run away and hide. The secret to success is suppressing that temptation and reaching within to find the drive to carry on.

How to see things through

Over the years I've heard plenty of stories from men and women who are now fantastically rich about the moments when they could have walked away. From their experience and my own, I've come up with a few techniques that can help you stick with it.

* Tell yourself it's OK to get despondent; after all, if it was that easy, everyone would be a millionaire. Having a bad day, or even a bad week, doesn't mean you'll always have bad days.

* Ask yourself what someone you admire would do in your situation. It could be Donald Trump, Alan Sugar or even Spider-Man, just think about how they would overcome the things that are troubling you. If you can imagine them coming up with a solution, then it means you are capable of solving that problem too.

* Ask for help. Is there someone you can talk things over with? Even if they don't have any relevant experience, sometimes having to articulate a problem can lead directly to you being able to solve it.

* Get out that piece of paper on which you wrote down what your business is about, what excites you about it and what you want to get out of it. Reconnect with your original idea: if you can tap into the dream, you'll be able to find the drive.

The best entrepreneur you can be

Your success will be determined by four factors: your attributes, your skills, your contacts and your environment. This next section is about identifying and maximising the building blocks of success that are all around you and, if you want to get a bit New Age about it, within you. At the end of this chapter, we're going to use the information you uncover in this next section to transform you into a perfect working prototype of an entrepreneur, so as you go through these exercises, make a note of anything you find out about yourself. Rather than me preach to you about your inner entrepreneur, I want you to do a bit of work and discover things for yourself that you might not have previously realised.

Part 1 – Your attributes

If you've never been in business before, or if you've never really been challenged in your working life, you can't expect to know what you're capable of. The exercise that follows has been designed to help you discover where your natural talents lie. I've always been somewhat sceptical about this kind of analysis, but I've actually found it quite revealing. It's also a bit of fun, and by working out what you're naturally good at, what you enjoy and what you're likely to excel at, it's easier for you to proceed with confidence. Similarly, if you discover that there are areas you're lacking in, then it enables you to employ people with complementary, rather than overlapping, skills.

Personality test

Completing this test is very straightforward. There are 28 pairs of statements. For each pair you need to allocate 3 points. You can give 3 to one statement if you agree strongly with it, or 0 if you absolutely disagree, or you can split the points 2:1. Just make sure that 3 points are always awarded to each pair, no more and no less. Sometimes you'll have difficulty choosing between statements, and sometimes your preference will be obvious. Just answer as honestly as possible. As you can see, each statement is followed by a letter. When you've finished, simply add up the points you've awarded to each letter.

1

When plans change, I am good at spotting the opportunities and
benefits of the new situation .... A
I'm good at knowing when the people around me have something
to offer .... B

2

I can get on well with anyone C
Being successful is more important to me than being liked .... D

3

I'm good at seeing things through to the end .... E
I come up with ideas for new projects easily .... F

4

I can usually figure out what will work best in most situations .... G
I am fair-minded and assess proposals on merit .... H

5

I come alive when new ideas and ventures are being discussed .... A
I find it difficult to take the lead C

6

I've been told in the past that I spend so much time looking at
the fine detail that I don't see the big picture clearly .... E
I like meetings and projects to be well structured and, ideally to
stick to the agenda .... H

7

I get frustrated when projects and meetings lose direction and I
try to bring them back on track .... D
I seem to have the knack of influencing people .... B

8

I don't like to come away from meetings until every viewpoint has been expressed .... B

I can be so objective about all the proposals I hear that I find it difficult to get excited about any one in particular .... G

9

I've been called pushy in the past. I think I was just trying to get the job done .... D

When I get excited about my new plan, it can be difficult to concentrate on anything else .... F

10

I'm useful to have around because I'm good at spotting little mistakes that other people overlook .... E

I think most people trust my judgement. If you asked people, they would say I was pretty fair .... G

11

I like to be the first to hear a piece of news or information .... A

I can liven up meetings by contributing something unexpected or original .... F

12

I'm good at seeing how ideas and innovations might benefit other people and other companies .... A

I have a talent for sticking to the brief and getting the job done ...... H

13

I don't like leaving loose ends. Some people call me a perfectionist ... E

I'm comfortable expressing unpopular views and will challenge people when I think they're wrong .... D

14

I am reliable and can be left to get on with the job unsupervised ..... H

I prefer working towards a common goal C

15

I like bouncing ideas around, just to see what gets sparked off .... A

My integrity and desire to do a job well mean I usually complete
projects on time .... E

16

I'm good at finding consensus and plotting a route forward .... B

My instincts are usually to go for the unusual option rather than
the safe one .... F

17

I'm useful for filtering out other people's unworkable or outrageous
suggestions .... G

I'm happiest at work when I'm using my imagination .... F

18

It feels good building friendships with colleagues and clients C

I've been known to prolong meetings and projects while I check
that everything has been done properly .... E

19

I think I'd only be happy working in a situation where I got to
meet new people .... A

I get satisfaction from properly weighing up all the options and
possibilities .... G

20

Although I like hearing what other people have to say, I never have
a problem making up my own mind .... B

I get pleasure from getting to know my colleagues and clients C

21

I really like to be able to devote myself to one project until it's finished .... E

I make good decisions under pressure .... B

22

I am pleased when I can solve a practical problem .... H

I've found I have the ability to influence opinions and decisions ..... D

23

When there are lots of people talking, I find it difficult to get my point across C

Explaining and clarifying detail is not my strong point .... F

24

Others may think I lack imagination or intuition .... G

I get a kick out of working with brilliant people, even if they can be difficult C

25

I'm good at bringing focus to projects that have lost their way .... D

I can keep my cool and think straight in stressful situations .... G

26

I work best when I have a clear goal or defined task .... H

I am comfortable asking people to do things that I cannot do myself .... B

27

I get bored easily and need other people to bounce off .... A

I get impatient when progress is slow or impeded .... D

28

When situations get difficult, I like to withdraw and take time to find a solution to the problem .... F

Sometimes I find it hard to get complex points across .... H

Now add up your score for each letter and write the totals in the table below. If your total doesn't add up to 84, go back and check your figures.

A	B	C	D	E	F	G	H	
+	+	+	+	+	+	+		= 84

Below are descriptions of eight different characteristics people display in their working life. The letter you've scored most highly in reveals your natural role at work.

Category A

Your strengths lie in research, investigation and diligence. You're great at preparing detailed reports, and your dedication to research can often produce effective solutions. Give you a brief and you'll beaver away at the task in hand until the aims have been achieved. You're a hard worker and you're good at keeping projects moving. However, you tend not to be imaginative, and co-workers rarely look to you for leadership.

Category B

You might get told that you lack a bit of flair or innovation, but you're very comfortable taking the lead. You make a good leader as you are both a natural collaborator and an assured decision-maker. You have excellent communication skills and are good at recognising other people's strengths. Your weakness is that you're not very good at working by yourself.

Category C

You're very practical. You like systems and targets, and are great at sticking to a plan. You have buckets of common sense and are a great team-worker. On the downside, you probably don't cope well with change and can become flustered and demoralised when goalposts are moved or plans change on the hoof.

Category D

You're great at taking someone else's ideas and bringing them to fruition. You're smart and grasp complex concepts easily and are often able to polish and improve on all aspects of projects. Although you have drive and self-confidence, you're not very vocal, which might mean you're not the most popular person in the office, especially when your frustrations at slower and sloppier co-workers come to the fore. You're very good at getting complex projects off the ground.

Category E

Your attention to detail can save a project from running aground. You are fastidious and are probably often called a perfectionist by friends and co-workers, who might sometimes think you hold them back by checking the small print. Nothing gets past you and you make sure deadlines are not missed. You probably wind up your more flamboyant co-workers, who see you as self-controlled.

Category F

You are the kind of worker who earns their keep with occasional flashes of brilliance. Your ideas and inventiveness transform projects and companies. You get a kick out of working on showy, headline projects and enjoy problem-solving. You are independent, imaginative and intelligent, and tend to think that all your ideas are brilliant. They're not, and you need people around you to tell you when your plans aren't worth pursuing. You can be impractical and are probably a bit of a dreamer.

Category G

You are a born analyst. You can assess and evaluate data, situations, problems and proposals. You're level-headed and can fairly weigh up several options. You tend to be cautious, some might say pessimistic and critical, but you're great at spotting where projects will run into trouble. Although you're probably not the greatest team-player, you are actually a vital part of any successful team.

Category H

You are great at implementation, but before you can get on with your work, you need to be convinced of the merits of the project. You like order, you like things to be put in writing rather than proceeding on a nod and a wink. You have buckets of self-control and oodles of common sense, but you have a tendency to be inflexible and unenthusiastic about new ideas.

How to use the results

Most people find they score highly in one category, with three or four categories tying in second place and just a few points left over for the remaining categories. Fairly obviously, the category you scored highly in reveals your natural strengths and attributes at work, and the categories you scored poorly in reveal the areas where you lack skills and insights. Although it's nice to know what we're good at, it's also very important to know where we fall short.

So how does this help you, especially if you're working on your own? Entrepreneurs tend to be an arrogant bunch – I think we have to be – but it does mean we don't always own up to our shortcomings, and this means that we can motor ahead without noticing the holes in our ideas, and our businesses. By knowing where your weaknesses lie, you can identify where you need to pay careful attention.

For instance, I've discovered I'm great at getting things off the ground and injecting momentum into new projects. What I'm not good at is seeing them through. These days, I pay people to implement my ideas for me, but when I first started, I had to be disciplined and force myself to complete tasks before I moved on to the next one.

If this exercise has revealed you're not naturally gifted at paying attention to detail, or seeing the big picture, or you've realised that you can be negative, it's important to review your fledgling business by role-playing from different perspectives. What would a perfectionist make of your plan? Or a doubting Thomas? Where might the skills of a creative genius get you out of trouble? Now you know where you're likely to stumble, ask yourself what checks and balances you can put in place to make sure you avoid simple mistakes.

I believe that it's always a good idea to look at your business from an outsider's perspective. Whether I'm planning to get a loan, or raise finance, or hire staff, I find it helps to imagine how other people will assess my company. I've also discovered that it's useful to see how an insider with a different set of priorities and attributes assesses my ideas. When Bannatyne Fitness is considering a new venture, I get two of my best employees – Nigel Armstrong, my MD, and Tony Bell, my director of projects – to play devil's advocate with each other to argue our options. Nigel is a bit like me in that he's inclined to take risks, but Tony is much more cautious. Their different perspectives are often poles apart, and listening in on their arguments tells me more about the opportunity in front of us than almost any other kind of analysis.

For me, the real benefit of this kind of personality exercise is working out who I need to surround myself with to make sure projects are a success. Whether you are in the process of assembling a launch team, or searching for a mentor, you should be looking for people with skills that complement yours. If you're a creative maverick, you don't want another one – you want someone who can soberly assess your ideas and help you deliver on them. If you're overly cautious, you want to team up with someone who's easily motivated.

The best ventures are those that make the most of all of these category types. If it's just you to start with, you need to make the effort to try to see your business from as many different perspectives as possible.

IIIIIIIIIIIIIIIIIIIIIIIIIIIIIIIII **CASE STUDY** IIIIIIIIIIIIIIIIIIIIIIIIIIIIIIIII

Name: Simon Woodroffe, OBE **Age**: 55
Job: Founder, Yo! Sushi
Qualifications: 2 O levels
www.yocompany.biz

One of the lessons I've learnt is that business, like life, is messy. Just as you can't plan your next girlfriend, you can't really predict how your career in business will work out.

I left school at 16 and went to Cambridge Tech to do my A levels. My parents probably hoped I'd become a military man like my dad or a stockbroker, but I never went to classes, so I never got any A levels and I became a hippy. I got busted for drugs when I was 19 and I was sentenced to eight weeks at Her Majesty's pleasure in North Sea Camp.

When I came out, I didn't know what to do, so I went to London and ended up answering an ad in *The Stage* for a stage manager's job in a tiny little theatre. It paid about 50p a day, but I eventually moved on to the Richmond Theatre. Although the work was hard and the money was crap, after a year I realised that I had actually learnt something, and that I had some useful skills.

Then I got into rock and roll, and if you knew your 'stage left' from your 'stage right', then you were seen as an expert. I started working with bands like the Sweet and Vinegar Joe, first as a roadie, then doing their lighting. I was freelance, but I regularly worked for the same companies and one day in the mid-1970s, I was in the office of a lighting company when they took a call from Rod Stewart's team. He wanted something different for his stage set, something a bit more like a West End production, and my employers needed someone who could pull it off. I said I would do it, and that was the start of my career in business.

At that stage, though, it was just an opportunity, not a business. I simply bought what I needed to buy, put it all together and got sent a cheque for the work. I used the lighting company's bank account for that first job, and when it was finished I carried on freelancing. I then got offered other work on the back of the Rod Stewart gig, and so I got my own bank account and set up SWA – Simon Woodroffe Associates – designing stage sets for rock concerts.

It was a bit shambolic, but when you're dealing with rock bands, they're all reasonably shambolic too, and if people thought you'd do a good job for a good price, then you'd get the business. I had the gift of the gab and I talked myself into contracts, but when each one ended, I always thought I'd never work again. I felt I was getting away with it, and it took a couple of years to build up any confidence in my abilities.

A few years later, I set up my first registered company, called S2, in partnership with a company called Norton Warburg that famously went bust with a lot of Pink Floyd's money. After that, I set up on my own and ran a company called Plumbline out of an office in Wapping, long before the developers moved in and made it desirable.

People think that if you start a business it's got to be perfect from the outset, and one of the lessons I learnt with Plumbline is that you can't do everything in advance. I hadn't got the VAT sorted out, or the accounts, but I knew fundamentally that if you've got the money coming in, then you're in business. I learnt to prioritise and I'd make lists of what had to be done. The first thing on the list was always to get the cheques in and make sure the show happened. When it gets to the stage that you need an accountant, then that's when you start worrying about getting an accountant. Eventually I learnt everything I needed to know about running a company, but at the start the important thing was just knowing where the money was coming from. Perhaps the biggest lesson about running a small business is cashflow:

if you run out of cash, then you run out of time, even if you've got clients and a track record. When I interview MBA graduates now, I often wonder what they really know about business.

I made a lot of mistakes, but the big one was trying to make as much money out of every contract as possible, and sometimes that was at the expense of doing the job well. That's when I learnt a really big lesson: that you're only going to get repeat business if you do your job well. It seems obvious now, but at the time it was too much hassle and I just took the money. I don't think I was ever very good at what I did in those days, but Plumbline did well enough to employ five people – me, a partner I had taken on, a secretary and a couple of designers – and gave me a decent income, probably the equivalent of about £100,000 today.

By the mid-1980s, we were pretty successful and we were asked by Harvey Goldsmith to stage Live Aid. There wasn't much of a budget because it was for charity, but it was good for the company's profile so we did it. It should have been a great time for me, but not long after Live Aid, I decided to walk away from it. I had fallen out with my business partner and I had also broken up with a girlfriend, so looking back, I can see that I was probably depressed. But that wasn't the only reason behind my decision: rock and roll had changed, and stadium tours were getting bigger and some really fantastic designers were coming on to the scene. I hadn't built a structure that could sustain that kind of competition, and the events we were staging were getting more and more stressful. We had these huge budgets to deliver huge shows, and something could have gone wrong on the road and I wouldn't have been able to respond. I thought I should get out before I was found out.

Looking back, I can see that I could have turned it around, but I didn't have a vision for the company. I saw us as an alternative rock and roll business, not something corporate, but now I can see that our skills could have been used to design restaurants – or anything else – as well as stage sets. At the time I didn't think about moving the business in that direction. I always had this little voice that told me I wasn't up to the job, and I believed it.

My decision to stop Plumbline coincided with meeting a guy who was making money buying TV rights for concerts from bands' managers, and I thought I could do that too. I had learnt quite a lot about deals and contracts from Plumbline, and the idea of not having to actually make anything was very appealing. So for the next seven years that's what I did, with varying degrees of success.

After a while, though, I missed the creativity of making things happen and started looking around for something else. Eventually I met a man who suggested opening a conveyor-belt sushi bar and my life changed again. I honestly believe that no matter how much physical preparation you do for a business – getting plans passed, finance raised or staff appointed – the psychological preparation is just as important. I would actually give equal weight to preparing your brain to preparing everything else, and with Yo! Sushi I was finally ready for success in a way I hadn't been before.

We are all a product of our upbringing, and I was held back by a limited belief in myself. I always thought that I couldn't be a really big stage designer for the biggest acts, and when I was in the TV business I always thought that I couldn't go out and do deals at the next level. The incredible thing I've learnt is that regardless of how high up you go and how big you think, there's actually no more work involved. If you think small, you get a small business; if you think big, guess what, you get a bigger business.

What's the best advice you've ever had? No one ever told me that the only way to make money from business is to create value. The problem with service businesses is that they're only as valuable as their next

contract, and that means they have no value to anyone but you.
What do you wish you'd known from the start? I love my life, so I wouldn't want to change anything, but knowing that I was a pretty competent person who was creative and capable of anything might have made a difference with my earlier ventures. Also, some decent tax advice: if I'd known about things like marginal tax relief, I definitely would have been better off.

What's the one thing you'd say to someone starting their first business? In the first two or three years you have to do every single thing yourself. I learnt to draw up accounts, PAYE, everything. But the only way to build a big company is to bring in management. When Yo! Sushi had four restaurants, the money was rolling in, but because I was running it, the money was also rolling straight back out again! I brought in a fantastic manager, Robin Rowland, who's really responsible for growing Yo! Sushi into the business it is today. I recognised that I'm an entrepreneur, which means I'm good at starting things: just as Robin couldn't have started the business, I couldn't have achieved what he has.

Part 2 – Your skills

As well as knowing where their natural abilities lie, it can also help new entrepreneurs to identify their skills. It's all part of working out what you're capable of, and I can promise that not only are you about to find out you are a lot more capable than you think, but that this knowledge will increase your confidence. And the more you believe in yourself, the easier it will be to convince others of your capabilities too. As with the last exercise, you'll also identify weak points that you can strengthen in advance, thereby making it less likely that your venture will hit a roadblock.

When I ask most people to tell me about their skills, they usually talk about their qualifications. 'I'm an accountant,' they say. So I ask them what else they do. I then find out that a woman who told me she was an accountant is also responsible for a team of 15, writes reports for her board and negotiates for her department's budget. So she's not just an accountant, she's a manager, an analyst, a writer and a negotiator. If I asked her about her activities outside of her job, I bet I'd find out about even more skills that were just as valuable as her ability to negotiate.

As entrepreneurs, it's not important how we answer the question 'What do you do?' What matters is how we respond to 'What can you do?' Some people tell me they're not qualified in anything. I don't believe them: when I realised I was the oldest beach bum in town, I also realised that – somehow – I had managed to pick up a motley assortment of skills without really paying attention: I had trained as a fitter and welder; I could work behind a bar (which involved a lot of mental arithmetic); I was physically fit (which meant I could work long hours); I'd worked out that if I got up early, I could get the best pitch on the beach and sell the most ice creams... I could go on. The point is that, regardless of our work backgrounds, we are all more skilled than we give ourselves credit for.

I've found that a good way to uncover the skills you don't know you have is, oddly, to write out your CV. Or at least a version of it, because this won't be a CV that anyone else will ever see – you're not trying to convince a prospective employer of your talents, just yourself. The reason why CVs work for this exercise is that they give you that little bit of structure to think about your life, year by year. It doesn't matter if you've never had a proper job. As you're about to find out, the skills you've acquired elsewhere in your life – from sport, from raising a family, from dealing with bureaucracy or anywhere else – are just as valid.

> **' As entrepreneurs, it's not important how we answer the question 'What do you do?' What matters is how we respond to 'What can you do?' '**

The longest CV in the world

Start by making a list of every area of your life – family, work, leisure, qualifications, childhood, travel, etc. Then break down each of these into the roles you've played within them. For instance:

Family	*Work*	*Leisure*
Parent	Welder	Watching sport
Partner	Team leader	DIY
Provider	Procurement	Pub
Cleaner	Planner	Boot sales
Disciplinarian	Union rep	
Bill payer		

Study	*Childhood*	*Travel*
NVQs	Sea cadets	Booking family holidays
Driving licence	Football	Extreme sports
	Bird-watching	

Now try to make the same list for different times of your life, possibly taking it year by year, and include your Saturday job when you were a teenager, the metalwork you got an award for at school and every job you've ever had. This will take time, but you should look at each of those areas of your life and write a CV entry for it. For instance:

Booking family holidays

Booking the family holiday each year requires coordinating all of the family's diaries to find two weeks we can spend together. It involves balancing our different needs – good weather, luxury, adventure, convenience and agreeing on a destination. I then research the travel and accommodation options and make the booking after agreeing a budget with my partner. I subsequently check visa, immunisation and insurance details, and closer to departure I supervise the packing and ensure we get to the airport on time.

Clearly, booking a holiday involves many skills. From this I can identify leadership, decision-making, administration skills, cooperation, negotiation and supervising. If this person also analysed the skills used in securing bargains at boot sales, the lateral thinking used in DIY projects and the ability to get on with a wide range of people in the pub and at football, then they start to seem capable of a lot more than their day job as a welder.

When you've finished your private CV, go through each of the entries and pull out all of the skills you've identified. Instead of seeing yourself as a particular type of worker, or expert, you should see yourself as someone with many skills. Hopefully, you can now see that you're able to approach a much wider range of tasks with confidence.

Part 3 – Your contacts

It's not what you know, it's who you know. I don't know who originally said it, but it's partly true. That said, I didn't have any contacts when I decided to go into the ice-cream business. I simply looked up 'Ice Cream Suppliers' in the Yellow Pages and talked to them all to find out who was offering the best deal. You don't need contacts to get a business off the ground, but if there are people in your life you can turn to for advice, information or maybe even money, then they can often make the difference between struggling for weeks on your own and swiftly making progress.

I believe it's worth taking a good look at the people in your life to analyse the things they know, the talents they've got and the contacts they have to see how their skills and knowledge can benefit your business. You may think you don't know a lawyer or an accountant or anyone who works in your chosen field, but they aren't the only people who can be useful.

Six degrees of separation

You've probably heard of this theory. It states that every person on earth is at most just six steps removed from everyone else. I should, therefore, be able to think of someone I'd like to have a meeting with, let's say the Director General of the United Nations, and someone I know personally will know someone who knows someone who knows someone who knows the Director General. We are all just a few phone calls away from anyone we need to help our business, so although you might not know anyone who you think can help, the chances are that one of your contacts – a friend, a colleague or someone from the gym – knows someone who could really benefit your enterprise.

An important thing to say about contacts is that it is often the people we know less well who turn out to be the most useful. If you think about it, it makes perfect sense. Often our closest friends will share the same circle of mutual friends, possibly drink in the same pub and do the same kinds of job in the same sector. Those we see less often tend to move in different circles, have different areas of knowledge and know a different set of people. So as you work through this section, remember that your contacts aren't just your friends, they are acquaintances, former colleagues, neighbours, even people you know from the pub, your plumber or the people in your mum's bridge club!

While you're going through these exercises, you should be considering if any of your contacts are so well connected, or so influential, that you should be tailoring your new business to make use of them. One of them might be your first customer, or someone who can introduce you to finance, or transform your fortunes in some other way. Your contacts are probably your most valuable resource, and it may turn out that you know someone with the power and influence to make a difference. If that's the case, you should try to find a way of incorporating their leverage into your launch plans.

Who do you know?

Take a look at your personal phone book and go through every name in it. Dig out your old phone book and read through the list of people you haven't spoken to for a few years. Scroll through the contacts in your mobile phone, your BlackBerry or your email account. Now grab your diary and scan through all the people you've met in the past year. If you've kept them, do the same with your diaries for the past few years. Think of all the different people you've met at events and parties, and start making a list of all the people you've had any kind of meaningful contact with in the recent past.

Now look at that list and ask yourself what you know about these people. What you're trying to establish is if anyone you know has a useful skill, area of expertise or access to someone with influence that could benefit your company. These are the sorts of things you want to know about your contacts:

* What they do for a living

* What they have previously done for a living

* What their hobbies and passions are

* Whether they have ever run their own business

* What circles they move in, and who they know that might be useful

By carefully thinking about the people who are only a phone call or two away, you should begin to feel more capable of pulling in the resources and help you'll need to make a success of your business.

From the list above, I think the most important factor is 'whether they have ever run their own business'. If you know anyone who's ever set up on their own, send them an email or call them up and ask if you could buy them a drink. So much of running a business is the same, no matter what line of work you do – hiring staff, finding premises, dealing with the VAT man, end-of-year accounts, health and safety compliance – that a local business owner is likely to have the names and numbers of lots of people who could help you.

Who can you get to know?

The world is full of people who could help you, and there are countless opportunities to meet them. Every industry has trade fairs, exhibitions and awards ceremonies, and you need to start going to the ones that are relevant to your business. Before you attend, you should be reading the relevant trade press for weeks, or months, to identify the key people in your field who you want to meet.

And it's not just industry-specific events that are useful. Your local chamber of commerce will hold regular events, perhaps your local council holds enterprise events, and even organisations like the Freemasons have a role to play in meeting people with a view to scratching each other's backs. I know plenty of people who swear the golf course is the best place to meet influential people. It never worked for me, but I probably went to the wrong sort of clubs! And don't forget online contacts. There might be discussion forums and chat rooms where you can make the virtual acquaintance of someone who could be a catalyst for your company. Many people now swear by networking sites like Facebook and LinkedIn.

People go to their industry's events to make contacts. It's often the case that the seminars, lectures and demonstrations are just a sideshow to the main event that happens at the bar afterwards. If you're new to an industry, standing like a lemon with no one to talk to can be daunting, but you soon learn that the other delegates are there for the sole purpose of meeting people who can further their career or profits too.

If you've seen someone give a speech, or read about them in the press, then congratulate them on their achievements, or ask them a specific question about their career. Tell them you're there to meet a lawyer/head-hunter/engineer and ask if they could introduce you to someone relevant. The thing about human beings is that, mostly, we want to help. Helping makes us feel good, and I know that if someone asks me something simple like a recommendation for a lawyer or the name of a helpful tax adviser, giving them a quick answer makes me feel better about myself.

Often these events will have delegate lists, and sometimes these will have the contact details of the attendees. These are incredibly useful resources and should be filed somewhere safe. Keep in mind that many of these delegates could be future employees, customers, clients or investors. Whenever you meet anyone new, ask them for a card, and then file that card where you can access it easily. Whether you keep paper or computer records, you need to start storing all the priceless data you'll harvest as you start networking.

I know some people whose single most important skill as an entrepreneur is their ability to network. They weren't all born with the ability to walk into a room and know everybody in it, and some of them have worked incredibly hard at it. One company director started off by keeping a scrapbook of contacts. He tore out profiles of people he admired from the trade press and stuck them in his address book. Then, when he was going to an industry event, he would look at the advance delegate list and compare it with his scrapbook. Can you imagine how flattered people were when he walked up to them and showed so much knowledge about their career and achievements?

This same guy now keeps a computer database of his contacts, and when he gets home from an event, he transfers all the details from peoples' business cards on to his computer. He doesn't just write in their job title and email address. He makes a note of their conversation. If someone tells him that they want to be a manager some day, when he reads in the trade press that his contact has been promoted, he'll send them a congratulatory email.

Needless to say, if you haven't already got yourself some business cards printed, you should do so straight away and make sure you always have them on you. This needn't be expensive: companies such as Good Print.co.uk offer 200 cards for under £20, VistaPrint.co.uk do it for free, and a Google search will find hundreds of others.

How to get the most out of your contacts

The more you can maintain your contacts, the more valuable they are to you. If you're the kind of person who is not too good with names and faces, then you'd do well to get a bit organised. When you meet someone at an event, always follow up that meeting with an email along the lines of 'I really enjoyed talking to you at the Expo. I thought your plans were fascinating and I look forward to watching your success over the coming months. You mentioned that you could let me have a contact number for your supplier. I'd be very grateful if you could forward it to me. Let's stay in touch. Best wishes...'

If you offered to pass on a phone number, or a press clipping, or anything else, make sure you do it. Whenever you send an email to a contact, you should make sure that your contact details are on it – phone, mobile, website, address, Skype, etc. – so that people have all the information they need to check you out and remind themselves who you are.

Even if you didn't meet someone at an event, it can still provide an opening to make contact with someone. 'Dear So-and-So, I had hoped to bump into you at the Expo last week, but our paths never crossed. I've long admired your work, and have already learnt much from your experiences since launching my own company three months ago. There was something I wanted to ask you... If I can return the favour in any way, just say the word.'

Most people like to help. If the occasional word of advice, or the sharing of the odd contact can hel, someone just starting out, then to do so validates their own achievements. Successful people are very unlikely to see you as a threat or a rival and will be interested in your business because they might be able to learn from it. Until you get to know people better, you need to make sure that your contact with them is professional and courteous. If someone doesn't know you very well and you bombard them with random emails or phone messages, you'll seem like a stalker and they'll back away! Whatever you do, don't start forwarding them comedy emails and YouTube links. Your contacts are not your friends, at least not yet.

More often than not, your most valuable contacts won't be the headline speakers at events, they will be the other delegates. The headline speakers probably get hundreds of people approaching them every year, and to be frank, they don't need you. The best contacts are those who need you too, and often these are other people at the beginning of their careers who need to swap information and contacts in return for something that will benefit them. Not only does this make for a more fruitful sharing of intelligence in the short term, but in the long term, when these people rise up the ranks and become major players, you will benefit from having known them a long time and from having established a meaningful, reciprocal friendship with them.

Reciprocal is the important word. The key thing about making and maintaining contacts is always to remember that what you can do for them is as important as what they can do for you. In the early days, it may be a bit one-sided, but as long as you start to repay favours over time, you will begin to get more and more out of your contacts. When you see an opportunity that isn't right for you but might be right for them, do the decent thing and tell them about it.

Part 4 – Your environment

Right at the beginning of this book, I talked through some of the common reasons people give me as to why they haven't started their dream business yet. A lot of the barriers – such as 'My partner doesn't support me' or 'I don't have the time' – fall into the category I call environmental barriers. Your environment plays an important part in creating the right atmosphere for starting and making a success of a business, and I think it's worth spending a bit of time looking at the things around you and seeing if there's anything that might potentially hinder your progress.

Every entrepreneur needs the time and space to work, and it's important that you know how you'll get both those things. You'll almost certainly need somewhere to set up a computer and some shelves or cupboard space for all your files and paperwork. I don't advocate spending money unnecessarily in the early days of a business, so unless you're already rich, you shouldn't be thinking of renting an office. However, you do need to figure out where you can work. If you've got a spare room, then that's fantastic, but if you don't, is there somewhere else at home where you can base yourself? The shed? Attic? A space under the stairs? An area that you can demarcate as belonging to your business and not your home can be extremely helpful.

In reality, most people have to set up a desk in the corner of their bedroom or work on the kitchen table. If you share your office with the rest of your family, then it becomes extremely important that you establish when the kitchen is your office, and when it returns to being the kitchen again. Your partner and your kids need to understand that at certain times of the day – whether that's after dinner or during the day – the room belongs to you and you need to be left alone to do your work.

As well as a physical space to work in, you might also feel the need to create some mental space in which you can think, problem-solve and experiment with different approaches. If you have a lengthy commute to an existing job, then maybe plugging yourself into your MP3 player could

111

get you the thinking space you need. Perhaps going for a walk, or even wandering to a quiet corner of your local library with a pad and pen might give you a chance to think.

Time to reflect on your ideas and your progress is a very important part of starting a successful business. You have so much to juggle on a practical level – meetings, accounts, customers, etc. – that unless you actually set aside some time for thinking, you might end up rushing headlong into the wrong thing.

Part 5 – Your team

Even if you are a sole trader and intend to work on your own for the foreseeable future, you will probably end up with a team of people around you who will help you get your project off the ground. I'm not necessarily talking employees or business partners here, just the friends and contacts you will rely on for advice and support.

Many businesses – especially many first businesses – are launched by small teams, often made up of the person who had the original idea and a few other professionals with key knowledge or skills. Some first-timers don't feel capable of setting up a business on their own and ask a friend to join them. In my experience, founding partnerships can be quite unstable, and more often than not, one person does 80 per cent of the work. I was actually in this position myself when I moved from the ice-cream business into residential care homes. It was a big move, one I didn't feel confident making on my own, so I went into partnership with a neighbour. We didn't work all that well together and I certainly didn't feel at the time that he had earned his 50 per cent share of the profits. However, looking back, I can see that he gave me the confidence to start a big business, and if that's all he did for me, then he was (just about) worth what the company paid him!

Whichever category you fit into – sole trader, partnership – understanding your team and your role within it could be crucial to your success. Some business books go into great detail about assembling the perfect team with the right balance of personalities, skills and experience. In my view, new companies are rarely perfect, nor do they have the time and money to recruit established professionals to clearly defined roles. Usually, they're built by people who happen to be around and are willing to take part.

When companies are started by friends, especially those that have previously worked together in the same field, you often find that certain skills are duplicated. What this means is that you may find yourself allocated to tasks that you are not naturally suited to, and that you may have to train yourself to get your head round bookkeeping, or VAT, or something equally dull while your partners go off to an exciting meeting.

In an ideal world, you would assemble a team made up of all the personality types described in the test at the beginning of this chapter. You would have someone whose natural tendency is to innovate, and another whose area of expertise is attention to detail, and another who is comfortable making important decisions under pressure. Rather than go into detail about team dynamics, I think it will be useful to look more generally at the roles most companies need to have filled. Depending on how you're set up, some of these roles will be fulfilled by employees or the launch team, or they may be looser arrangements with people outside your company. In reality, I suspect that you yourself will undertake more than one of these roles.

The leader

Every new business needs someone out front who leads with passion, vision and commitment. Ideally, they should also be a great manager, but in the early days, what's really needed is someone who can keep pushing forward, someone who is so focused on the goal that they carry everyone else around them with them. This role requires the ability to be self-disciplined, to make decisions and to make sacrifices: for many months, possibly even years, the business will be the most important part of their life.

The administrator

New businesses tend to move so quickly that paperwork and bookkeeping can often get sidelined while important meetings and targets draw the team's focus elsewhere. The role of administrator is crucial as a business that does not keep simple accounts can't possibly know how well – or how badly – it's doing. In many businesses I know, this role is carried out by the founder's partner or a useful family friend. It doesn't need to be a full-time role in a new business, and can easily be carried out by the founder – as long as they ensure that they set aside the time to do it properly.

The technician

The technician is the person who is closest to the product or service you produce. It may be that they invented the thing you sell, or that they are involved in its assembly, but they are the person who plays with it, refines it, tests it and irons out problems and glitches.

The salesman

This is the person in your team who is closest to your customer. This person's job involves understanding what your customer needs and how they will use and benefit from whatever it is you offer. This person will be constantly finding new ways of getting close to your target customers and uncovering their desires so that he or she can better target your marketing.

The workers

Ultimately, every business has to get on with the day-to-day delivery of the product or service you provide. These members of the team need the time, the tools and the support to do the work that provides everyone else with an income.

The mentor

This can be one of the most important positions in a new company and often it is taken by someone who is not involved in the everyday running of the business. Starting a new venture is demanding and daunting, and even the most able operators need someone they can talk to. Mentors can be wives or husbands or friends down the pub, but it's such an important role that you should give some thought to appointing someone to the position. Ideally, your mentor will have skills, knowledge and contacts that can make your job easier. If it's someone who has been involved in a start-up venture before, then so much the better as they'll understand what you're putting yourself through. Formalising this relationship – perhaps by giving them a couple of per cent of equity in your company – means you won't feel that you're taking up their time and benefiting from their expertise unfairly. A good mentor will challenge your assumptions, play devil's advocate and give you a hard time. While it's nice if they can sympathise, what you really want is a different perspective that can help you solve problems and keep moving your business forward.

IIIIIIIIIIIIIIIIIIIIIIIIIIIIIIII **CASE STUDY** IIIIIIIIIIIIIIIIIIIIIIIIIIIIII

Name: Kanya King, MBE
Job: Founder, MOBO Awards
Qualifications: O levels, A levels, kicked out of Goldsmiths College,
later received their fellowship and a business doctorate from
London Metropolitan University
www.mobo.com

Ever since I can remember I dreamt of being a part of an event like
MOBO. I didn't necessarily want to start it, I just wanted to be there
and enjoy it! Music was a big part of my childhood – my older sister
started taking me to gigs when I was just 12 – and most of my friends
were musicians. I started putting on music nights when I was 17, not
really to make money – I was happy if they washed their faces – I just
wanted to help people I thought were amazingly talented and to
create the kind of events I wanted to go to.

Throughout my early twenties, I became increasingly disillusioned
with the fact that the music I liked wasn't getting the same recognition
as pop acts, despite massive record sales. I started writing to the big
music companies and talking to all the existing awards shows to see if
they would incorporate more of the music I was into. I told them there
was a massive audience for this type of music, but they weren't very
receptive at the time. At some point I thought that if I wanted this to
happen so much, I needed to do something about it and put my
money where my mouth was.

I'd always had some little enterprise on the go: while at school, I usually
had a part-time job, whether it was getting up early for a paper round,
selling whistles at Notting Hill Carnival or doing odd jobs. As one of
nine kids, if you wanted to wear nice clothes you had to earn your own
money, so where I could find work, I would take it. It was a pretty crazy
household – my mother's Irish, my father was Ghanaian, and there were

five of us sharing a room sometimes – so you learnt to speak up if you didn't want to be invisible, and you soon realised that people were far more likely to help you if you were polite, courteous and forthcoming.

I got my O levels and A levels and went to Goldsmiths where I studied English and drama. I eventually got kicked out because I didn't attend enough lectures: I was busy with my son and the events as well as other pieces of work. I got a job as a researcher working on a show for Carlton Television, coming up with programme ideas and sourcing guests. I was never responsible for anything financial or legal, and even though I always worked, I never acquired those kinds of useful skills. I didn't know anyone who had started their own business and no one in my family could help with official things. I used to tell my mum about some of my ideas and she'd always find 101 reasons why I would lose money and shouldn't do them!

However, I had made the decision to create a new sort of awards show, one that would be an umbrella for many musical genres, even incorporating new ones as they emerged. I knew that if it was going to be successful, it had to have a really good name. I remember sitting round my kitchen table with a group of friends in early 1995, and we eventually agreed upon the name MOBO. It was perfect – not only was it short and memorable, but it sounded a bit ethnic and it felt right. The phrase 'music of black origin' also encompassed everything that I wanted it to include and, above all, it was not exclusive, not just for black artists. I wanted the awards to demonstrate how black-influenced music continues to have a major impact on the mainstream, as well as inspiring much of what is fresh and innovative.

I loved the name, but when I started talking to people about it, they thought it had something to do with mobile phones! I realised I needed to launch the idea properly to raise its profile and build up momentum. I decided I would throw a launch party at the Ministry of Sound and knew I would have to fund it myself.

I was very fortunate as I had bought my first property when I was young and had discovered a bit of a passion for property, and had started to build up a small portfolio. I was able to remortgage and release £15,000. It represented an awful lot of money to me then, but it was still a tiny budget for a professional launch party. So I called in every favour I could, got artists I knew to wear T-shirts saying how much the MOBO Awards were needed and asked friends to help me on the night. I booked the Ministry for a Sunday because it was cheaper, but I then realised how hard it would be to get journalists and the media there at the weekend. But I was committed, so we just kept asking people. I was working from home and I'd be walking around in my pyjamas taking these really important phone calls, but somehow we pulled it off.

We got good coverage in papers like the *Observer* and TV exposure on *London Tonight*. The coverage was so strong that I went to talk to TV companies about broadcasting the ceremony, but there was a reluctance because they thought there wasn't an audience for it. LWT expressed some interest, but they had just commissioned something similar. However, someone there put a call in to Carlton TV – their 'rival' in London – just to check that they weren't doing anything with us, and although Carlton had already turned us down, it was enough for them to pick up the phone and call us back in for a meeting.

They said, 'We've got good news and bad news. The good news is that we're going to give you a transmission slot, but the bad news is that it's in six weeks' time and we've only got a little budget.' I couldn't believe it – I wasn't planning to have our first event for a year! However, I knew I had to say yes and that somehow we would put the event on in their timeframe.

Our first show cost about £60,000. Carlton gave us a small budget of around £25,000 and I put in more of my own money. I was also fortunate that one of the doors I had knocked on in the early days was a company that gave me office space. They also lent the MOBO organisation money that would not need to be repaid immediately. I knew putting in more of my own money was a risk, but I also felt that it was better for me to do this and make a mistake than not to do it at all. I told myself that if I could learn from it, then I could make future events a success. Only those who dare to fail greatly can ever achieve greatly.

I got a few friends to work with me and four of us organised the whole event. The only venue we could afford at such short notice was the New Connaught Rooms and even though we were doing it on a shoestring, I was determined that the MOBO Awards would be a glamorous event. I wanted people to dress up, I wanted well-known people there, I wanted to overturn the negative perception and stereotypes.

We had so many doors slammed in our faces when we invited people, but we said to them, 'Would you allow us to update you on our progress?' So whenever an act agreed to perform or attend, we called these people back, and our credibility grew with every phone call. We asked Tony Blair, who was leader of the opposition, and Cherie to come. His office had said no all along, but then a couple of days beforehand they said maybe, and eventually they were keen to attend.

We lost money on the first event, but my response was to say, 'Right, what have we learnt? What can we do better? What do we have to change?' We had so much coverage that I knew that the following year's event would be bigger and better. Nevertheless, there was no money around and so I went back to work to pay our overheads. We had such a positive response from the community that I knew the MOBO Awards were not just about the music. It was a social movement too and we became a voice arguing for better education and better representation. It had never been about the money, and we developed community action projects alongside the awards events.

In our third year, we got a network slot on Channel 4 and we moved the event to the Royal Albert Hall and we've never looked back. We are now involved in events all over the world and get global coverage for our flagship show. The events are profitable, but the real value is in our brand, which I've paid a lot of money to protect – we've registered every trademark we can think of in many different classes. We even get unsolicited approaches from people wanting to invest in our brand, our magazine, our new social networking site as well as our community initiatives.

What's the best advice you've ever had? My mother told me that where advisers are many, plans succeed – meaning, do not rely on advice from just one source.

What do you wish you'd known from the start? I relied on the help of friends, some of whom I employed, for the first few years and one of them became my accountant. Unfortunately, that didn't work out well, and I wish I had paid for solid professional accountancy. Also, I wish I'd learnt to say no more often. As a beacon organisation we are constantly asked for help, and at one stage it started to affect my own business and my health, devoting so much time to these requests. I have a much better balance now.

What's the one thing you'd say to someone starting their first business? I didn't have a mentor in the beginning; I didn't have anyone to talk to. I now have a board made up of people with a variety of backgrounds and different areas of expertise. It is important to have that kind of support.

‖‖‖

4 The plan

If you've never been in business before, there's a pretty good chance that you've never seen a business plan and might not be all that sure what they're for. You're not alone: I hadn't heard of one until a bank manager asked me for one!

A business plan is a document that sets out the reasons why the business was started and the reasons why it will be a success. Generally, the plan serves two purposes: to help you (and your management team if you have one) plan the growth of the new company, and to persuade investors to part with their cash. It conveys the company's exciting prospects to potential backers while simultaneously motivating and focusing the people running the company. These are two very good reasons why writing a business plan is a productive use of your time.

At this point, I want to say something to those people who are reading this and thinking, I don't need a business plan. I'm going to skip this chapter. It's true, if your business involves no more than your effort and your money, you might feel you don't need to spend the time writing a business plan. However, there is a lot of information in this chapter that I believe will help every business achieve its aims. Absorbing the points I make here will help you identify problems and maximise opportunities.

If you put 'business plan template' into Google, you will get tens of thousands of results and you can see plenty of examples of what other companies have produced. You'll also find several people offering to write your business plan for you – and charge you an arm and a leg for it. In my opinion, there are two exceptionally important reasons why you should never outsource the writing of your business plan: a) you'd be showing poor financial judgement by paying for something you can easily do yourself and, more importantly, b) you'll understand your business much better if you write it on your own.

Even if you are not planning to seek finance from banks or investors, I think it can really help new entrepreneurs to write their business plan as if they need external finance. This imposes a rigour to the assumptions you make and encourages you to accomplish the task with professionalism. Banks and investors will ask questions about your assumptions and forecasts that can find flaws and faults you might never otherwise uncover – until you run into trouble.

I asked my bank manager to help me write a business plan for my first nursing home as he knew what his head office would need to see in order to approve the loan that I wanted. Together, we took my basic calculations of 'so much per resident per week minus costs' and came up with something that convinced his bosses I was worth the risk. For me, it was an interesting exercise in understanding how banks viewed new ventures and it helped me anticipate some issues with cashflow that I might otherwise have stumbled over when we were up and running. However, I don't remember ever looking at that business plan again. Most people do, though, and it can be useful as a kind of map against which you can measure your progress.

Just as looking at your business through the eyes of an imaginary, or real, lender can give you valuable perspective, I think it can also help to imagine how shareholders, a chairman and employees would see your venture, even if your enterprise is fairly modest. Think carefully about how they would view the moves you're making, and ask yourself if the problems they would raise are things you need to address immediately.

Most business plans I receive from people who want me to invest in their company are around 20 to 30 pages long, and most of them follow what has become a pretty standard format. Following this format gives you a template to work with and ensures that you don't overlook any important aspect of your business. Structuring your business plan needn't be difficult: use clear headings, start each section on a new page, and don't go over the top with eye-catching fonts and innovative layouts: it's the substance not the style that matters, and there's always a chance that it will format differently on someone else's computer (it's likely you'll be emailing it, rather than posting it). For that same reason, use a basic file format (.doc or .pdf is standard) as anything created in an unusual program is less likely to be readable at the other end. The other thing I would say is, don't rush it. It shouldn't take up too much of your time – perhaps an hour a night for the next fortnight – and once you're finished, re-read it, spell-check it and then give it to a friend to see if they can make sense of it. It's important that someone with no previous knowledge of your venture can get a clear picture of your plans from this document as that's the position an investor will be in. If they are confused about anything, keep refining it until your message is crystal clear.

As you start to write your business plan, I'd encourage you to see your first attempt as a rough draft. In fact, it's really just a draft of a rough draft of the first draft: you don't need to know everything at the outset, and you'll return to it and refine it as you learn more. If you include the following sections, you can feel confident that your business plan will paint an accurate picture of your ambitions for your company.

1 The pitch

This is sometimes called the 'executive summary' and is essentially a few paragraphs that sum up what your business offers and why this is exciting. If you are seeking investment, this is what you initially send to potential backers and if they are sufficiently impressed, they then ask to see the rest of the document. Your executive summary is therefore the most important part of any business plan and it's worth taking your time to get it right. Be warned, though, if it's a shameless bit of PR puff or an obvious sales pitch, investors will see right through it. What we want is a genuine assessment of the opportunity you're offering us.

I like business plans to start with an 'elevator pitch' – basically, what you would say to Bill Gates, or me, if you bumped into us in the lift and only had ten seconds to convince us not to get out at the next floor. It can be incredibly difficult to condense your entire vision down to one sentence, but doing so really focuses your mind on what you're doing and why you're doing it.

An elevator pitch should convey what you do, what you stand for and why someone should take you seriously. If I were to give you an elevator pitch for Bannatyne Fitness, it would probably go something like this: Bannatyne Fitness operates the best health clubs in the best locations for 18- to 80-year-olds. If I was to do it for Quality Care Homes, the nursing-home business I started in the 1980s, it would have read: Quality Care Homes offers private bedrooms with en-suite bathrooms and first-rate care for the elderly at the same price as other operators provide shared bedrooms without toilet facilities.

You might want to pull out that piece of paper on which you wrote down the reasons why you were starting this business and the things that excited you about it. Is there something there that can help you develop a winning elevator pitch?

In the next sentence, I want to see three things: I want to know how the business makes money, why you want to do it and why you're the right person to make a success of it. There are then seven other points you need to get across in your pitch:

1 A brief overview of the opportunity that the company has been set up to exploit

2 The company's origins and its strategy for exploiting the opportunity

3 An outline of the size and characteristics of your market (i.e. your
  customers)

4 Profiles of the founder and management team, explaining what
  particular talents and skills they offer the business

5 A picture of how the business will grow

6 The amount of money needed to launch the venture

7 The expected profits for the foreseeable future

You will return to all of these points and expand on them throughout the
rest of the document. When you've finished your business plan, return
to the pitch and make sure it gives an accurate account of what is to follow.

2 The idea

This section doesn't have to be long, but I want to know what your idea is
and why there's a business in it. I want to see how you solve your customers' problems and understand how that produces a profit.

I don't want to read how you sat round in the pub and came up with
the idea after two pints, but I do want to understand why you think there's
a demand for your offering. It's a very good idea to include examples of
similar businesses in other locations and explain why you think you can
replicate – and improve – on their business models.

I want to see as much detail about your product or service as you have,
especially if it's an invention. I need to understand what makes it attractive
to your customers and why they would buy it from you and not somebody
else. Obviously, where appropriate, I want to see that you have all the
relevant patents and trademark applications in place.

You should include data on how much it costs you to produce your
offering, and how much you can charge for it. You should also say how
this compares to similar products available elsewhere.

3 The market

This section is all about who's going to pay you for your product or service. It may be a few weeks, or even several months, since you did the initial fag-packet analysis of your idea, and if that's the case, the street surveys and word-of-mouth enquiries you carried out into your market probably need to be revisited. Be prepared to alter your business model if the information you uncover now differs from those initial findings. This is the sort of information you need to provide:

Market size

You need to know the size of the current market, and if there are any factors that may see the size of that market increase (or decrease), such as demographic change or access to technology. There are a number of ways you can determine the size of your market. If you have a general product for the mass market, then you can use information from the last census. National data is available from the Office of National Statistics (www.statistics.gov.uk), while local data is held at neighbourhood libraries. If you're aiming your offering at a particular group of people – say epilepsy sufferers, nurses or school children – then this information will be available from a relevant charity, union or government department. The circulation of relevant magazines and user numbers of appropriate websites can also indicate the size of your market. If your business aims to serve a particular town, be realistic about how far people will travel to use your business. If you operate online, include figures relevant to the web and not to the market in general. This is also the place to add in information you've gathered yourself through street surveys, etc. For example, you might say, 'In addition, we have also carried out our own survey of local shoppers, and eighty-seven per cent of the people we asked on a Saturday afternoon said they would use our service.' Add as much detail as you have, and make sure it is presented clearly: investors will be looking for concrete data about your market.

You need to give a reasonable prediction of the size of your market –

and please note my use of the word 'reasonable'. We've had so many people come on *Dragons' Den* and say, 'It's a billion-pound industry. If we can get just one per cent of the market, this will be a huge business.' Market share in this context is meaningless, and if you put something like that in your business plan, you'll look like you don't know what you're talking about. Personally, I've never felt the need to predict my market share: when I opened my first nursing home, I only cared that I could fill it with residents. I care about the size of my market, not my market share.

However, this plan is meant to help you anticipate the likely size of your business, so you need to apply some common sense and find ways of predicting how big your business will be. Rather than picking a figure out of thin air, it actually makes sense to start by working out what your capacity is. Let's just say that you're starting a window-cleaning round. You are capable of cleaning the windows of three houses an hour, and you are going to work ten hours a day, six days a week. That means you can clean 180 houses a week. Assuming that each householder wants their windows cleaned once every eight weeks, that means you have a total possible number of customers of 180 x 8, which equals 1,440 houses. Now if there are 10,000 houses in your town, that means you are aiming for just under 15 per cent of the market in your area.

Another way of calculating your likely market share is by looking at a similar business. If you have been modelling your idea on a business you've seen in operation elsewhere, then you could reasonably assume that you will achieve a similar market share. You could also adjust that figure if you have a larger sales force, a better product or some other competitive edge. Likewise, if you have a smaller sales force, or a poorer location, then you need to revise that figure downwards.

❛ *I care about the size of my market, not the size of my market share.* ❜

Your customers

Your customers might not be familiar to your potential backers. Say you want to start a service for the racing world, it's unlikely an investor will have a detailed understanding of your niche market of owners, trainers, grooms and jockeys. I therefore think it's important to set out some biographical data about your customers, perhaps even adding a couple of case studies. You need to be able to show that these people really need your business and that they are likely to respond well to it. If you've already been trading for some time, use testimonies from your existing customers.

The competition

Who else is competing for your customers? List rival companies, giving their size, their profits (this information is available from Companies House, if it's a limited company, or from the stock exchange if it's a plc), their location and how long they've been trading for. Set out their weaknesses and how you will compete against them.

4 Revenue streams

Unsurprisingly, this is the section a lot of investors will turn to first. You need to list all the ways in which your company will make money. If you're an online retailer, for example, in addition to the profit you make on your transactions, you might have an additional income from advertising. If you're a retailer, you may also have an online presence, or offer mail order. If you're starting a PR agency, you'll make some money from individual campaigns, but some clients will keep you on a monthly retainer. However you earn your money, separate out the different revenue streams, and as you do this, consider whether there is a way in which you could maximise that source of income. At Bannatyne Health Clubs, most of our income comes from our membership fees, but we also make an income from our shops and cafés and from one-to-one training. What are your additional sources of revenue?

5 Marketing plan

You need to set out how you are going to reach your customers. Will you advertise in the local paper, use a viral email campaign or put leaflets through doors? Or might you use a combination of all three? Perhaps you can set up affiliate deals whereby other companies that send business your way get a fee (this is a very well-established way of reaching new customers online). In this section, itemise all the tools you will use to reach your customers together with the costs of each method and the timeframe in which you will employ them.

6 Operating plan

You and your investors need to know how you will achieve your aims on a practical level, and in this section you need to explain how you will put your plan into action. The kinds of things I would want to see here are who you would hire, when you would hire them, how much you would pay them, the command structure and an explanation of how you provide your service to your customer. A flow diagram of the likely progress of your company can also be very handy, for instance:

Set up website
▼
advertise
▼
after 100th sale, rent office
▼
after 200th sale, hire staff
▼
when tunover hits £1 million pa, set up 2nd branch

You should aim to include as much detail as possible about the catalysts and targets that will move your business forward. You can break it down into months if that helps show your planned progress more clearly.

7 The team

Some people just cut and paste the founders' CVs in here, but I think you can do a much more persuasive job by singling out the attributes, experience and skills that will allow you to make a success of the venture. If your work history is relevant, then you should of course include your past jobs, but if you're entering a new field, then highlight the transferable skills you'll be taking with you into your new role – specific expertise, proven problem-solving ability or financial know-how. Do this for every key member of your team, or if the company is just you at this stage, then I want to see the names and addresses of suppliers such as your accountant, your lawyer or any other relevant expert. If you have a mentor, then include a couple of paragraphs about the benefits they bring to your company.

8 Financial forecast

This is the business end of your business plan, and the data you supply here could make the difference between getting financial backing and failure. I've already said it a couple of times, but you really will find running a business much easier if you can become confident with spreadsheets. You don't need accountancy training, and probably spending an hour or two with the manual that came with your software – or with an online tutorial – will be sufficient.

I suggest that you prepare a cashflow forecast for your first two years of operation. Month by month, tally up your costs, then enter your likely revenues. Deduct one from the other and carry your profit – or loss – forward. What follows is a simplified version of what's required for your first year:

Month	1	2	3	4	5	6
Fixed costs						
Rent	0	0	800	800	800	800
Utilities and rates	40	40	120	120	120	120
Variable costs						
Staffing	0	0	2000	2000	2000	3000
Manufacturing	600	600	1800	1800	1800	2400
Distribution	100	100	300	300	300	400
Subtotal	740	740	5020	5020	5020	6720
Revenues						
Sales	500	500	1500	1500	2000	4000
Affiliate income	0	0	50	100	250	500
Subtotal	500	500	1550	1600	2250	4500
Monthly profit	-240	-240	-3470	-3420	-2770	-2220
Accrued losses	-240	-480	-3950	-7370	-10140	-12360

Month	7	8	9	10	11	12
Fixed costs						
Rent	800	800	800	800	800	800
Utilities and rates	120	120	120	120	120	120
Variable costs						
Staffing	3000	3000	4000	4000	4000	4000
Manufacturing	2400	2400	2400	3000	3000	3000
Distribution	400	400	500	500	500	500
Subtotal	6720	6720	7820	8420	8420	8420
Revenues						
Sales	5000	6000	7000	8000	10000	14000
Affiliate income	600	1000	1200	1500	1500	1700
Subtotal	5600	7000	8200	9500	11500	15700
Monthly profit	-1120	280	380	1080	3080	7280
Accrued losses	-13480	-13200	-12820	-11740	-8660	-1380

What can you tell me about this business from this spreadsheet? I'll tell you what this sparse data tells me:

* The business starts small and doesn't move into premises until early sales figures indicate the project is likely to succeed.

* The increase in the staffing figure tells me staff are only taken on as and when the expenditure can be justified.

* The amount of money it needs to raise is £13,480, which is the maximum accrued losses in Month 7. After that, they start to repay the investment from monthly profits.

* By the end of the first year, the debt is nearly paid back, and in Month 13, you would expect this business to have cleared its debt and be making a significant monthly income in excess of £7000.

Although this seems like a robust, if small, business, I wouldn't automatically trust the figures, as I would want to test the assumptions the founders have made. I'm not quite sure I believe that they can steadily build their sales figures like that without having a budget to spend on marketing. I'd also need to understand the way in which the revenue from 'affiliates' is calculated and would expect to be able to turn to a page in the business plan that sets out how their affiliate scheme works. If something isn't immediately clear from the figures, then whoever is reading it should be able to find the supporting information easily elsewhere in the document.

If you are supplying your spreadsheets on disk, or as an email attachment, the chances are any investor will play around with the figures and carry out their own sensitivity analysis on your business. As you haven't done this since your fag-packet calculation, it's time to do it again and you should include some altered scenarios in your plan. Repeat the previous cashflow but put your costs up by 10 per cent, 20 per cent and 30 per cent, and reduce your sales by similar margins to show how robust your business is. If you find that you go into the red with only a small adjustment, you will find it very difficult to raise finance.

In addition to including a month-by-month cashflow, you should also include a projection of likely future growth, year by year, following the same template. For instance:

Year	1	2	3	4	5
Costs	150000	70000	90000	100000	110000
No. of sales	300	600	1200	2400	4800
Revenues	45000	90000	180000	360000	720000
Profit	-105000	20000	90000	260000	610000
Accrued profit	-105000	-85000	5000	265000	875000

* In this example, I can see that there are exceptional start-up costs, as the costs in Year 2 are less than half what they were in Year 1.

* Sales double every year, and revenues increase accordingly.

* I can see that at the end of the first year of trading, this company is £105,000 in the red, and that by Year 3 it has broken even (the £5000 figure at the bottom of the Year 3 column).

* By Year 5, this company is producing a healthy profit in excess of £600,000 a year.

As long as these calculations seem plausible and are based on assumptions explained elsewhere in the document, then this forecast gives an investor – whether that's someone you're asking to put money into your business, or someone whose time and expertise you intend to exploit – a picture of the sort of business they're getting involved with.

Be warned: when you do your forecast, do it logically. There is a temptation to extrapolate early successes and assume that growth will always be constant. In reality, there is a natural size to some businesses, and once the local market is saturated, the business objective stops being expansion and starts being retention and protection.

The simplest way to impose a reality check on your forecast is to look at your total sales figure for the fifth year. Let's just say that, like the business in the last example, you sell a total of 4,800 gizmos. What do you have to do to sell that many gizmos? If your line of business is one where your sales team have to make 100 phone calls to make a sale, that means your sales team will make a total of 480,000 phone calls a year. Now calculate how many calls they can reasonably expect to make in a day. Let's say it's 25: that means 19,200 selling days in a year. Clearly there aren't that many days in a year so you need to divide it by the number of days an average worker works each year to find out how many sales reps you need, and that's roughly 230. Which means you'd need a sales staff of 83. Is that very likely? What are the cost and rent implications of such a large sales force?

There are only 168 hours in the week, and that's if you operate 24 hours a day. If you are going to run a shop and will be open from nine until six every day apart from Sunday, then there will only be 54 commercial hours in your week. Look at your figures, and see if it's really plausible that your team can achieve everything you are promising in the time available. If it doesn't ring true to you, it will be making a clanging noise in any potential investor's ears.

I hope this gives you a little taste of how dangerous spreadsheets can be. You have to study the business behind the figures, and check if it's the business you had in mind, or if it's a ludicrous fantasy.

These days, detailed spreadsheets are usually sent as a separate email attachment or on disk. For your main business plan, select the headline figures, and condense all the financial information into a couple of key paragraphs that paint the overall shape of the business.

9 Exit strategy

If you are seeking investment from a venture capitalist or an angel investor (the different types of finance are explained in the next chapter), then you need to be able to offer your investor a return. I am amazed at how many people come into *Dragons' Den*, or send me their business plan, and don't tell me how I will get my money back – with considerable interest. An 'exit strategy' is the means by which an investor can expect to realise their investment.

If you aren't planning on seeking investment, I think it can be helpful to think now about your future plans for your business. Are you hoping to sell it for millions, or hand it on to your children, or issue licences for franchises? The reason I want you to think about this now is because it's an important part of being an entrepreneur. So far I've talked a lot about 'entering' business and not too much about 'taking' the profits (remember, that's what an entrepreneur does). Realising your investment – the fruits of your ingenuity, time and labour – is the pay-off for working so hard. However you are funding your venture, knowing what your exit strategy will be is fundamental.

There are traditionally three ways in which the equity in a company is released, and you should work out which suits your company best.

IPO

This stands for Initial Public Offering, which is another way of saying 'stock market flotation'. When companies are floated, a percentage of their shares are sold to the market, and these usually include the shares allocated to your investor. So let's just say that I invested £500,000 in your company for 25 per cent of the shares. When you float your company for £20 million, I would sell my shares, which would now be worth £5 million. Smaller companies can be floated on AIM, the Alternative Investment Market, where there is less regulation and you don't need to provide two years' worth of accounts. Of course, you don't have to sell just your investors' shares; you can sell some of your own too and take your first step to becoming seriously wealthy.

Not all companies are suitable for flotation, and this is only something you should put in your business plan if you think yours is the kind of company that is capable of creating that kind of wealth. If not, you might like to think of some of these other exit strategies.

Selling the company

Companies are bought and sold every day, often to their competitors or another company who might profit from their expertise or access to customers. Sometimes companies are bought to be closed down because the purchaser wants to put them out of business! Is your company likely to be of value to another company? If so, then this could be the right option for you to put in your plan.

A management buy-out

This means exactly what you would expect it to: the management team buy out the investors. Once a company is making a good profit, you can take out a loan to pay back your investors and use the cashflow to repay the loan. This can be an excellent strategy as it gives you cash and help when you need it, and in the long term doesn't leave you at the mercy of markets and brokers.

How to use your business plan

When you've written your business plan, read it at regular intervals. In the early days of a new business, it is easy to get distracted, and a business plan that has been thoroughly thought through can act as a virtual mentor.

While it's a very useful tool for keeping you in touch with your original intentions, you shouldn't look at it as something that is set in stone. As you learn new things, develop new products or make new contacts, the path of your business could subtly, or seismically, shift. When this happens, you should adjust your plan accordingly (while making sure to label your new plan appropriately using v1, v2, v3 suffixes to denote which version you are using. It also helps to add the date to each version).

You can even alter your business plan depending on who you are sending it to. Your bank might ask for very specific information, and different investors have different investment criteria. Before you send anyone your business plan, you should make sure that you meet their benchmarks. These are often on the company's website, but if not, they are never usually more than a phone call away.

Remember, your business plan will often act as an ambassador for your business, and when people read it, it is likely to be the first they will have heard of your venture. It's therefore absolutely crucial that it is always well presented, whether you send it by email or by post. Spell-check it, double and triple check your figures, and make sure any attachments are included. You'd be surprised how often people overlook the basics. Unsurprisingly, if an entrepreneur gets simple things wrong in their business plan, an investor is inclined to wonder what other simple things they will overlook.

|||||||||||||||||||||||||||||||||||||| **CASE STUDY** ||||||||||||||||||||||||||||||||||

Name: Chris Gorman, OBE **Age**: 41
Job: Serial entrepreneur
Qualifications: 5 O Levels
www.chrisgorman.com

Born and bred in Hartlepool, I left school in the early 1980s when unemployment among school leavers was running high at 22 per cent. Times were changing and the town's traditional employers – in ship-building, steelworks and coal mining – were losing contracts thick and fast and so there just weren't the jobs that a kid from a poor back-ground like mine might once have got.

As a teenager, I had to develop my formative money-making skills as my family couldn't afford pocket money. For example, I quickly realised I could make more money organising the paper rounds for the newsagent than delivering the papers for him. And then, when I had a milk round, I realised that taking a bit of time to talk to the customers meant I got bigger tips. Regardless of the local difficulties, on leaving school I had ambition and I talked my way into a management trainee job at the local Fine Fare supermarket. I was paid £36 a week, which was barely enough to live on, but I wanted to be my own man and so I moved out of home into a bedsit. I found out that the branch manager was earning £35,000 a year, and this motivated me to work hard with the goal of earning that kind of money myself one day.

When I was 18, I had what I can only call a life-changing moment. I found a copy of Dale Carnegie's *How to Win Friends and Influence People* lying around in my building. I didn't have 50p to put in the electric-ity meter and couldn't watch TV that evening, so I decided to read the book instead. It was a revelation; I didn't go to sleep at all that night. I read the book cover to cover and even though it had been written in 1936, it still seemed so relevant to me. It's all about achieving what you want out of life and it made me realise that I wanted more, and that I wanted to be wealthier. One of the lessons in the book is that you should regularly assess your progress, take the time to figure out what's working, what's not, and what you want. Its basic message is that to achieve your full potential you should invest time in *yourself*; and for me it paid dividends.

Within a couple of months I got a new job as a sales rep for Text Lights, the scrolling red LED signs that were very popular in shop windows in the 1980s. I travelled all over the country selling them, and discovered I was very good at sales. I regularly took home £200 a week, which created a massive change in my circumstances. This motivated me even more and I began to formulate my goal of becoming a millionaire by the time I was 30.

When I was 19, I moved to London and got a job with a small mobile-phone retailer, managing one of their shops. I was very successful there, which led to a job with Vodafone and earnings of around £60,000 a year. I bought myself a flat in South London and thought that life couldn't get much better. But then I met my wife, Mary, and it did!

When Mary got pregnant with our first child, Blair, we decided to move to Scotland to be near her family, and this presented me with the first really big financial challenge of my life. I had bought my flat for £80,000, but the market had collapsed and it was now worth £60,000. Our minds were made up – we were moving – so I had to take out a loan to pay the shortfall and we moved into a council flat in Cumbernauld, £20,000 in debt.

For the next two years I worked incredibly hard at Securicor's mobile communications division, eventually paid off the loan and we went on to buy our own house in Renfrew.

I transformed the fortunes of Securicor in Scotland, and the company was keen to give me a promotion in London, but I knew by then that I wanted to stay in Scotland, and I'd also started thinking that I wanted to work for myself.

I had been reading personal development books, like Anthony Robbins's *Awaken the Giant Within*, and I was looking for a new challenge. One of my clients was a new mobile-phone dealer called DX Communications, run by a young guy like me called Richard Emanuel. Richard had also read Robbins's books, and we decided to go to one of his three-day seminars in Chicago together, doing the fire-walking bit and everything! While we were away, Richard asked me if I'd help him build the company.

Everyone, apart from my wife, thought I was crazy. I had just cleared my debts and not only was I giving up what was now a £70,000 a year salary, but I borrowed £25,000 to put into the business. I was also going to be taking a pay cut – to around £25,000 a year, which meant Mary would be the main breadwinner for the next four or five years.

However, I never saw it as a risk: I saw it as an opportunity. I knew I could sell very well, and if it all went wrong, I figured I could easily get another sales job. My investment meant I owned 30 per cent of DX Communications, Richard had 40 per cent, and another partner, John Whyte, also had 30 per cent. John was older than us, and was great at the operational side of the business. Richard managed the business while I drove the sales and marketing. Together the three of us made a pretty good team and we're still the best of friends today.

I had worked in mobile phones long enough to know that the future was in retail, so we opened our first shop in Pollokshields in Glasgow, and over the next five years we expanded rapidly, eventually opening 170 outlets. We didn't know much about running a company and we made a lot of mistakes – we hired cheap staff rather than the right staff, and we could have struck far more favourable contracts with customers – but we were lucky: the mobile-phone business was growing so rapidly that new cash was constantly being thrown into the industry, and this kept us going at times when we probably should have gone under.

It was pretty chaotic and exhausting; we were always robbing Peter to pay Paul and begging for more time with our suppliers. After about two years, the business needed to borrow more money, and the banks asked for our homes as security. Mary was pregnant with our second child at the time, and I didn't want to worry her, so I didn't tell her what I'd done. I always meant to tell her, but the business started to do well again and there didn't seem to be any risk.

Inevitably, though, we had a cashflow crisis, and we needed emergency funding. We were turned down by everyone, and I remember lying awake all night working out how I could tell Mary the bank would repossess our house, wondering if we'd be able to move in with my in-laws and then realising I'd be out on my ear for not telling her in the first place!

Thankfully, we got a loan from the Bank of Scotland, and we weathered the storm. That said, we still knew very little about keeping accounts, or our responsibilities as directors. People said we were over-trading and we didn't even know what they meant. Of course, it meant we were expanding too quickly and were very vulnerable. I was never that worried, though; I always thought we were in the right business, and I always knew the business would succeed.

In 1996, when I was 29, the business was flying and we sold a 25 per cent stake to Cellnet (now O2); my share of that was £1,070,000. I have framed the bank statement that shows the money transferred into my account – my balance went from being £4,000 overdrawn to a balance of £1,029,000 once the lawyers had taken their cut. I had done what I'd set out to do. I had become a millionaire a month before I turned 30.

It was a wonderful moment: we had all worked so hard, putting in 70- and 80-hour weeks for almost six years, and now we had achieved financial security. In 1999, we sold the rest of our interest in the company, which by then was valued at £42 million.

In the years since, I have started a series of businesses – I'm now involved in around nine – and although I've made a lot more money since, that first million is still special.

What's the best advice you've ever had? At DX, when we had about six or seven shops, we wrote to Sir Tom Farmer, the founder of Kwik Fit, and he told us something that I've never forgotten: *it's all about people.* You have to remember that your staff have lives outside work, and sometimes they might have had a bad day, but the more you under-stand your people, the more you get out of them. Treat them as you would a friend, be there when they need you and make them feel like they're on the inside and involved in decision-making. Companies don't succeed, *people do.*

What do you wish you'd known from the start? Always pay for the best people you can find.

What's the one thing you'd say to someone starting their first business? It doesn't matter how focused you are, you've got to find the right people and inspire and motivate them, and make sure you share your vision with them. Communicate with them: if you're not a great leader, you won't achieve what you want to.

5 Raising finance

By now you should know how much money you will need to get your venture up and running, and this chapter is about working out the best way for you to get hold of the necessary funds.

I'm going to take the different options in the order I think are best from the entrepreneur's point of view. I'll start with by far the best way to fund a business – putting your own money into it.

DIY

Obviously, if you've calculated you need £1 million, then this probably won't be your preferred option, but as most businesses can be started for a few thousand pounds, I believe it is the best way to fund the majority of new companies.

There are two very good reasons why self-funding is my preferred route. Firstly, it means you only have to please yourself and are not pressured into making a decision because either your lender or your investor wants you to adopt a certain stance or demands repayment. To put it succinctly, you retain control. Secondly, if you put your own money into it, I'm damn sure you'll work a lot harder to make your business a success.

If you can't raise enough money on your own and are reluctant to borrow, then you also have the option of cutting your cloth. Can you return to your business plan and incorporate your limited access to funds into your launch plans? Can you start smaller and re-invest early profits so that expansion is funded by revenue? Sometimes the rigour imposed on new businesses by cash constraints can really focus the founders on core activities, rather than getting distracted by spending investors' money on peripheral items. Funding your growth this way means you build very strong foundations for your future empire.

Not all of my suggestions will be feasible for everyone, but by using a mixture of various sources of cash, you can avoid the time-consuming process of applying for loans or pitching to investors.

Sell your assets

What do you have that's worth something? Your car? Your flat screen TV? Your vinyl collection? We live in affluent times, and even the moderately well-off have homes stuffed with gadgets, appliances, furniture and collectibles that could be sold to raise cash. You don't necessarily need to live without a car, just sell your valuable car and buy a much smaller and older car. Similarly, as you won't have time for watching DVDs, ditching the home-cinema equipment for a second-hand portable TV shouldn't be too much of a wrench.

I've been told there's a TV show called *Cash in the Attic* on which, day in, day out, the presenters manage to flog the participants' trinkets at auction for thousands of pounds. Have a good look round your home – including sheds and attics – and see if there's an heirloom you could turn into cash on eBay.

Britain is a nation of homeowners. Over 70 per cent of properties in Britain are lived in by the people who own them. This means many of us have access to quite a serious amount of cash, if we are prepared to sell our homes. This isn't something anyone should do lightly, but if you're absolutely sure of your business, and have absolute faith in your figures and projections, then you might reasonably assume you'll be able to buy a much bigger house in the near future if you do. Of course, moving to a smaller house is another possibility.

Cashing in investments

According to National Savings & Investments, the average amount of cash saved up by Brits – excluding pensions – is a whopping £18,705. This money might be tied up in ISAs, premium bonds or 60-day-notice accounts, but it's not that difficult to free up. Think about all the places you have put your rainy-day money and ask yourself if it could produce a much better return if you put it into your business.

Nearly a million Britons are now landlords and have second properties they could sell. Even more of us have some kind of investment in the stock market. Perhaps it's time to liquidise those assets – and turn them into cash.

Releasing equity

You don't have to move to get the money out of your property. If you've lived in your house for at least a couple of years, the chances are that you have several thousand pounds of equity in your property. Assuming your credit rating is OK, you could remortgage for a few thousand pounds more than your current mortgage and invest the difference in your company. Your mortgage payments will go up, of course, but as they will typically be spread over 25 years, this is an affordable way of raising cash.

Hopefully, through a combination of these sources, you'll be able to raise enough cash to get started. Even if you have ambitious long-term goals for your business, this is the best way to get off the ground. Aside from retaining control and being more motivated to recoup your investment, there is a third reason why self-financing the early days of a business is the best way forward: it impresses investors.

I am far more likely to invest in a company if the founding entrepreneurs have already invested in it themselves. Not only will I be impressed by their commitment, but because the business will have been in operation for several months, I can see the beginnings of a track record before I part with my money. Banks take a similar view: if you've got accounts for six months' worth of trading that demonstrate financial aptitude, they will be more likely to offer you a loan at a good rate.

Borrowing from the bank

Some of the biggest fights of my career have been with bank managers: I've been convinced it's a sure thing, and they've begged (incorrectly, as it turned out) to differ. Despite these debates, I still believe that borrowing from a bank is the best way to get your start-up costs met if you can't raise the funds yourself.

If you need less than £25,000, you can usually get a loan (ideally, an unsecured loan) without having to tell the bank what you need the money for. If you'll need more than that, then you'll have to jump through a few hoops. Whatever the amount you need to borrow, if you're about to get yourself into tens of thousands of pounds of debt, I think it's important that you understand how banks work. As with every negotiation in business, you're in a stronger position if you can see things from your adversary's point of view. The two things that might not be obvious to a first-time entrepreneur are that a) banks have strict lending criteria and you need to be able to tick all their boxes for them to say yes, and b) banks don't take risks. As long as you understand those two things, you can usually get what you want out of your high-street lender.

Box ticking

Each bank has slightly different lending criteria, and your own bank might be a little more amenable to your request for a loan if you have a good track record with them. Before you send your business plan to any bank, pick up their literature and ask their new business manager (every decent-sized branch has one) what their lending criteria are. Then simply tweak your business plan to make sure it demonstrates how well you stack up against their targets. The kinds of boxes banks like to tick are: good credit history, previous trading experience, sector experience and that the size of loan required is in proportion to the opportunity (i.e., they're not going to lend you £30,000 if your business plan suggests you only need £20,000).

Generally, the more boxes you tick, the easier it is for junior and local managers to approve your loan. If you've got a patchy credit history or are asking for a lot of money, it's more likely that the manager you speak to will have to refer the decision higher up the bank's food chain. Sometimes, arranging a loan can take weeks, if not months. The smaller the amount, and the better track record you have, the quicker the process will be.

Risk intolerance

If you send your brilliant business plan for your brilliant business to a bank, there's a decent chance they'll lend you the money. However, a bank will ask for something in return – security. Even if it's impossible for your business to fail, a bank will want you to offer your car, your home or anything of value against your business going bust. As one bank manager said to me, 'We're not a bookies!'

If you don't have a home or are unwilling to offer it as security, then a bank might refuse your loan, even if they have faith in you and the business. If your bank smells the slightest whiff of risk, you might be asked to pay a higher rate of interest or have some other onerous clause attached to your loan. They might ask for a guarantor – a home-owning relative or friend who is willing to put their property up as collateral in lieu of yours. The thing you must never forget about dealing with the banks is that if you default, they will do everything in their power to get back the money they lent you. They will seize your assets and auction them off to whoever offers them enough money to repay their loan. If you're lucky, there might be something left over that they'll return to you, but they really don't care about your financial well-being, only theirs.

I'm sure you're familiar with the phrase ' No risk, no reward', and just as the riskiest ventures tend to produce the best financial rewards (as well as the highest number of failures), by minimising their exposure to risk, banks are able to ask for very little return. Which is why – despite the obvious personality clashes between entrepreneurs and bank managers – banks and new businesses make such a good fit. Basically, you take the risk, and you get the reward.

Let me give you an example why I have no qualms about borrowing from banks. Let's say I borrow £50,000 from a bank at 7 per cent interest over ten years. My monthly repayments will be around £580, and at the end of the ten years, in total, I will have paid back around £69,000, which means the bank will have made £19,000 out of me. However, at the end of those ten years, I could have a business worth millions of pounds, and all it's cost me is £19,000. If I had got my finance from any other source, it would have cost me an awful lot more.

When I first started, the only banks I had heard of were the ones on my local high street. Although these are the banks that most of us tend to have a relationship with, there are hundreds of other smaller banks that have to compete with the high-street names. They can't compete on visibility or high levels of awareness, so they compete on deals. If you look at the tables in the money section of your newspaper, you'll see the best loan deals on offer that week, and these are rarely from the names you recognise. Use a website like www.moneysuper-market.com and you'll see even more banks you've never heard of. Not only do these banks tend to have the best products, but they have much better customer service, and I find it far easier to speak to a person in a branch than a temp in a call centre. Just make sure that the bank you are dealing with has signed up to abide by the Financial Services Authority's regulations.

Not only are interest rates generally competitive, but banks don't ask for a stake in your company and, once the loan is paid back, you still own 100 per cent of your business. So why don't I suggest you just borrow, instead of selling your possessions first? That way you could launch your business and keep your car and your flat-screen TV. I guess it's just common sense – not only do you impress the banks with your commitment, but the less you borrow, the lower your repayments will be and the less of a drain they will be on your cashflow.

Just as people get into personal debt by borrowing on a credit card to pay off their overdraft, that is repaying a loan, inexperienced entrepreneurs can find themselves in difficulty trying to meet the bank's monthly repayments. It may be that your business needs to spend six months in a research-and-development phase before any revenue can be produced and, if that's the case, you need to know how you will meet your loan repayments in the short term. If your revenue is erratic, your repayments won't be a problem some months, but could give you a terrible headache in the other months.

Whenever you take out a loan, ask for funds to be made available on a 'draw-down' basis. In practical terms, what this means is that the bank agrees a loan, which it will make available to you, but if you only spend that money gradually, you will be only charged interest on the money you actually withdraw. The following illustration shows how much money this can save you:

Loan amount	50,000	50,000	50,000	50,000	50,000
Amount used	10,000	20,000	30,000	40,000	50,000
Monthly repayment	**116**	**232**	**348**	**464**	**580**

Interest rate: 7 per cent. Loan period: 10 years.

The only reason not to take your money on a draw-down basis would be if you could find a savings account that was offering a higher rate of interest than your lender is charging you. This occasionally happens with introductory deals, but it's very rare and the gain is so small it's probably not worth the bother when there are so many other things for a new entrepreneur to focus on.

Finally, I think there is one other benefit to getting finance from a bank: you build up a reputation with them, and at some point in your career, you will need the banks. You might lose an order, have a client go under or any number of disasters that can cripple even established businesses, and when that happens, your good standing with your bank might be what keeps you afloat.

The better your relationship with the banks, the better the interest rate they will offer you. When I invested in Igloo, the refrigerated logistics company, on *Dragons' Den*, one of the first things I was able to do for them was broker a better deal with their asset lender. Overnight, the founders had several thousand pounds a month being invested in their company rather than inflating their lender's profits.

Of course, when you talk to any bank, you should investigate what other offers they have for new businesses. Some will offer free banking for your first year and your own business manager. Don't be swayed by offers to put your logos on cheques or a lovely plastic ring binder for your statements – go for the bank that saves you the most money.

Pros and cons of borrowing from a bank

Pros	Cons
You don't give away equity	It can take weeks to make a decision
Relatively low interest rates	They will want your house as security
You build up credibility for the future	Repayments are a drain on cashflow

---

Other sources of lending

If you don't tick the banks' boxes, then there are several other sources of lending out there that might be suitable for your needs. It might also be that you need additional funds to supplement an existing loan from a bank.

Friends and family

Some people would call this section 'Friends, family and fools' because when you start telling your nearest and dearest about your plan, they might get so excited about it, and become so convinced of its money-making capabilities, that they offer to put some money into the business. Obviously, not all of them are fools, but don't get too carried away when those closest to you tell you you're a genius. However, when you run out of cash and need to find money from somewhere fast – friends and family can be very quick on the draw.

Needless to say, borrowing from friends can be fraught with misunderstandings and mixed expectations. Firstly, as amateur lenders, they probably have unrealistic expectations of the returns they can expect. Usually the only time new businesses make the news is when they become overnight successes, and consequently the general public sometimes think that they can put a few grand into a start-up and end up a millionaire a couple of months later. Therefore, you have to lay some ground rules.

1 Establish whether you are taking a loan, or whether they see their money as an investment in return for equity in your company.

2 Agree a fair interest rate and decide if the loan is to be repaid monthly or in full at some specified future date.

3 Never accept money that you think they can't afford to lose. It's one thing being motivated by the thought of losing your own cash, but the thought of losing someone else's money can be crippling and

could colour your decision-making. Don't ask anyone to gamble their house or their pension on your venture, no matter how sure you are about it.

4 Agree whether or not their money gives them any say in the way in which you run your company. What would happen if you want to take it in a direction they don't agree with? What kind of voting rights, if any, are you prepared to give them? Personally, I wouldn't give them any, and if they didn't accept my terms, I would find another source of money.

5 You have to be sure that they have accepted they are taking a risk. If the company goes bust and their money is lost, they should not have any right to seek compensation from you.

Credit cards

When I built my first nursing home, I couldn't get a loan to cover the building costs, and so for months I juggled my builder's bills with various credit cards. I didn't see it as too much of a risk because I knew that as soon as the property was built, I could get a mortgage on it that would pay off the credit companies. If you choose this route, then you need to be very sure how you will pay off the debt, because if you don't, the high interest rates charged by credit companies will soon see you in real trouble.

That said, buying things on credit cards has obvious advantages for a new business with cashflow issues. You can buy something on 1 February and won't get your bill until the end of the month. You probably then get another fortnight to pay the bill, and if you pay it off in full, then it won't cost you anything. Wherever possible, avoid getting cash out on a credit card as the interest charged on cash advances can be eye-wateringly high.

Many credit-card companies offer interest-free introductory periods, and if you're good at managing your money, then this is obviously an extremely good way of borrowing. However, if you're not on top of when the introductory rate expires, or any limits on your spending, then you could see yourself lumbered with hefty charges. If I have one rule about using credit cards, it's 'Use them, don't let them use you.'

Credit cards can sometimes be advantageous over other forms of lending, especially if you only want the cash for a short period. Unlike some loans, they don't have arrangement fees or early repayment penalties. And if you already have a credit card, it's not unusual to be able to call up your credit company and ask for an extension on your credit. Most will run a credit check while you're on the phone and (assuming your credit rating is OK) they will extend your credit limit there and then. It's probably the quickest source of borrowing, and there may be days when that is more valuable to you than a slightly better rate.

> ❛ *Use credit cards, but don't let them use you.* ❜

Grants

If your business has an ethical purpose, then there's a chance you might be eligible for a grant. While all sorts of businesses can qualify, if you're a social entrepreneur I believe it's well worth finding out if you're entitled to assistance, because the beauty of some grants is that, unlike loans, they don't have to be repaid.

The government makes money available through countless organisations with the aim of encouraging enterprise. The Small Business Unit within BERR, Business Link, the Department for Innovation, Universities & Skills, DEFRA, the Industrial Development Board in Northern Ireland, the Scottish Executive, the Welsh Assembly and most local authorities throughout the UK consider giving grants to organisations that will be creating local employment, preserving a trade in danger of being lost, helping the environment, creating new export opportunities or offering services to children, the vulnerable or the disabled. The EU also has a grants scheme.

As you can imagine, some of these bodies can be inundated with applications, but there are some that don't advertise very much and if you master their box-ticking exercises, you stand a surprisingly good chance of getting some of their cash. Be warned, though, grants are rarely for the full amount you need. Typically, they offer 50 per cent of your start-up cash if you can prove that you can match their funds. It's also not uncommon for grants only to be made for specific projects rather than general running costs. They have another disadvantage in that the application process can be very drawn out: in some cases, decisions might not be made until the end of the financial or calendar year.

Grants come in several different forms. The most common is a one-off payment, but some organisations offer interest-free loans (or subsidised loans), or will take an equity stake – but at a much lower level than a commercial investor would.

Each organisation has its own criteria for acceptance and the secret to getting grants is understanding exactly what the grant-giving body has been set up to achieve. You need to find out what their aims and objectives are and then find a way of conveying to them how your business helps them achieve their aims. There's no point approaching an organisation that aims to help young entrepreneurs if you're over their age limit. Similarly there's no reason why a grant organisation hoping to increase public participation in sport through grants would give money to a business in any other field.

There are so many sources of grants that finding out what you are entitled to can be a time-consuming task, and you will have to approach several organisations to get all the information you need. Ask for any leaflets or background documents the organisation has produced and study them to see if a) the application procedure is a good use of your time, and b) if your business meets their criteria.

My best advice is to start with the Business Link website at www.

businesslink.gov.uk, where there is a searchable database of sources of grants, but I would also advise doing an internet search for something like 'grants for new businesses' to see what else is out there. If your business is likely to be eligible for lots of grants, you might want to investigate using a grants consultant. Believe it or not, there are people who spend all their time filling in forms on behalf of other people, and if that lets you concentrate on your business, paying their fee might be worth your while.

How to maximise your chances of getting a grant

Apply early
If you can be among the first to apply for a new grant, competition for funds will probably be less and those administering the scheme will want to show their bosses they're doing something.

Do your research
Talk to the grant-giving body before you apply and get advice on what they want to see. Make sure you meet their criteria.

Stay informed
New grants are launched all the time and the criteria for them change frequently. Once you've made contact with a grant organisation, get on their mailing list and stay up to date.

Tick those boxes
When you fill in your application forms, ensure you make it clear how your business fits in with their stated aims and objectives. If you can show that you match their criteria, you make it much easier for them to award you a grant.

Lay it on with a trowel
Tell the awarding body that you *need* their cash and that your business, which will increase tourism, provide local jobs, preserve traditional skills or

whatever else they've been set up to fund, won't go ahead without their support. Give them a chance to be your hero!

Show them your business plan
Let them see what an organised, thought-through and cunning business you will be able launch on the back of their award. Give them the big picture.

Prove you can match their funds
As most grants will demand 'match funding' from another source (ideally your own pockets), make sure you can show that you will have the money in place.

|||||||||||||||||||||||||||||||||| **CASE STUDY** ||||||||||||||||||||||||||||||||

Name: James Caan **Age**: 47
Job: CEO, Hamilton Bradshaw
Qualifications: Graduate of Harvard's Advanced
Management Program
www.james-caan.com

I came from a business family, and I knew from the age of 12 that I would start my own business at some point. Business fascinated me, and the thrill of the deal, of success, was as exciting to me as music or football was to other people. I put entrepreneurs on pedestals because I thought that making your money from business was more sustainable than being a popstar or a footballer, and that through business you could build a platform that could take you wherever you wanted to go, whether that was into the House of Lords or on to another venture.

As a kid, I would look at a brand or a business, and I'd wonder what made the owner come up with that name, or figure out what advantages they had.

My father's ambition was that I would join the family business, and until I was about 16, this was something I didn't question. But by the time I was 18, I couldn't see where the challenge was and it just didn't interest me: it was too easy, so I started looking for a business idea that I could develop myself.

I didn't see the point of getting qualifications. The way I saw it, I could spend five years getting A levels and going to university, and only end up doing what I knew I was going to do anyway. I decided getting experience of work would teach me more.

My father was in textiles, and I would buy and sell merchandise that he had produced. I bought samples from the manufacturers, packed them in a suitcase and went to Ireland to walk the streets, selling to shops door to door. It made me realise that I wanted to be in a professional business, with a nice office. I could have made money out of many of the ideas I tried, but if the idea doesn't suit you, then you won't see a future in it. I had an image of myself in a large city building wearing a good suit, and I was in search of an industry that could give me that.

I was attracted to the recruitment industry for a few reasons. Not only was it based in an office, but it was Monday to Friday, and so many businesses, especially retail and leisure, are six, if not seven days a week. I also liked the fact that the remuneration was incentivised: if I placed a lot of candidates, I would get the rewards.

I worked for a couple of agencies, and then as a recruitment manager for a firm that employed recruitment agencies. I got to know the industry very well, and I discovered a gap in the market. At the time, in the mid-1980s, there were essentially three sorts of agencies: the high-street companies like Brook Street and Alfred Marks that did general recruitment up the £30,000 salary bracket; the mid-range companies that did selection for middle-management positions by placing advertisements in newspapers; and the executive search agencies, or head hunters, at the top end, who filled senior roles.

The gap I spotted was this: in the mid-range, the agencies charged a fee, typically 25 per cent of the candidate's first-year salary, and then charged for the advertising on top. By adding the cost of the advertising, they often worked out more expensive than the executive search option that charged 30 per cent, and if no decent candidates replied, then the advertising money had been wasted. My idea was to bring head-hunting to the mid-market, which made perfect sense to me, as for every chief executive, there are ten middle managers to recruit.

When you're looking to set up a business, you have to have a differential: there's nothing special about an opportunity when you're another 'me too' business in a highly competitive market. I knew finding a differential was fundamental to success, and I was convinced I had found it. If Step One in starting a business is having the idea, then identifying your differential should be Step Two. For me, recruitment wasn't that exciting, but the differential *was*.

The next step was creating a brand. I wanted to start an elite business for top-end customers and candidates, so I needed to create a brand that fitted that market. I wanted something that everyone assumed already existed, something that said gravitas, substance, integrity and professionalism. I put myself in the mindset of potential clients, and asked myself what characteristics they would want to deal with, and I came up with the name Alexander Mann.

I also wanted a classy location, and even though I didn't have any money, I walked up and down Pall Mall, where the Institute of Directors is, to see if anyone would rent me a room. I told the manageress of a serviced office company that I had a budget of £100 a week. She told me, 'This is Pall Mall, not Petticoat Lane!' But she managed to find me a tiny room with no window, where you couldn't open the door without it hitting the table. I didn't mind: I got to put Pall Mall on my business card and that was what I wanted. Of course, there was no room to interview people in my office, so I would meet candidates in reception and say: 'I'm really sorry, but all our meeting rooms are full. Would you mind if we just pop down to Claridges for a coffee?'

I was 24 and had a couple of thousand pounds saved up, which was enough to keep me going while I sat in that broom cupboard with a Yellow Pages calling financial services companies and introducing 'our' mid-range executive search service. People found it genuinely interesting, and after about six weeks, I picked up my first assignment. I filled my first position four weeks later, and the moment the cheque came in, I went down to reception and said, 'I'm ready for my new office, and this time can I have a window?'

In my fourth month, I hired my first employee, but I knew nothing about National Insurance or payslips. I called up the PAYE helpline, but when all the paperwork arrived I couldn't understand any of it. At the end of his first month, I simply went down to the cashpoint to get the wages out and put them in an envelope. I called a friend, who in turn knew an account, who I called for advice. He offered to come in one Saturday a month and do all my paperwork for me, so all I had to do was keep my receipts and invoices in an envelope, and he would write everything up for me. I learnt early on to surround myself with people who complemented my weaknesses. You don't have to be an expert on everything.

The first couple of years were tough, as we were a new business offering a new service, but by 1987 our profit was £450,000, in 1989 it was £600,000. In 1991, however, during the recession, I remember sitting with my accountant doing our annual accounts and realising that we had made just £1,500 in profits. The recruitment business mirrors the economy, and we were hit hard: I didn't see the point in continuing. For about six months I really neglected the business as I looked around for something else, and Alexander Mann started to nose-dive. But at the end of those six months, I realised that I understood recruitment and I had a greater chance of success with the business I already had than something new, so I threw myself back into it, and we began to thrive. We moved into IT recruitment, and sales and marketing, and eventually we started recruiting for the recruitment industry, something which no one had thought could be done. When I sold part of the business in 1999, we were charging £130 million in fees annually, with some of our profits diverted into backing other start-ups which have also become multi-million-pound businesses.

What's the best advice you've ever had? Observe the masses and do the opposite! My father told me that, and it's true. The herd mentality means everyone wants to be in the same place, but if you go into a crowded market, you dilute your business. When everyone's going in the same direction, it's often the road that leads the other way that's paved with gold.

What do you wish you'd known from the start? Honestly, not a lot. Whatever you do, you just have to find things out for yourself. Although, when I got to 40, I began to wonder if I had missed out on something by not going to university. I wouldn't change anything, but I did enrol at Harvard Business School when I took a year out after I sold Alexander Mann, and I had a great time.

What's the one thing you'd say to someone starting their first business? It's all about execution, and not about the idea. People come to me with ideas all the time, but it's not ideas that succeed in business – it's good execution. The second thing to say is that business is about a team: no one is an expert on everything, so be just as conscious of the things you don't know as the things that you do, and hire to plug the gaps. Also, don't be afraid to hire people who are better than you: eBay was a good idea, but the best thing the founders did was hire Meg Whitman, who has turned it into the business it is today.

Business angels

A business angel, or angel investor, is typically a self-made entrepreneur who invests their cash and expertise in new companies with the intention of getting a good return. All of the Dragons are business angels, and it won't surprise you to hear that I think angel investment is a great idea.

If you're going to look for investment in your business, then the first thing you need to understand is the risk-reward ratio. The banks hardly take any risk, and they're happy if they make a couple of per cent on their loan. Business angels take a much bigger risk, and therefore they look for a much bigger reward, usually around 20–25 per cent of the amount they invest but some look for 50–100 per cent.

An angel will typically invest between £50,000 and £250,000 in a new business, but that's not the reason why angel investment is so prized – as well as their money, you get the angel's contacts, expertise and guidance as part of the package. Often, an angel will take on – officially or unofficially – the role of chairman to the founder's chief executive. If your angel has experience of the sector in which your business operates, then so much the better.

However, there are two potential downsides to angel investment for budding entrepreneurs. The first is that some angels have been known to take over. If they've sold their businesses for millions, there's a chance that they miss the cut and thrust of commerce so much that they can't resist getting overly involved. This doesn't necessarily spell disaster, but it might not be what an entrepreneur wants.

The second possible pitfall to consider is that angels often ask for quite a large slice of your company, and this is one of the reasons why so many people have left *Dragons' Den* without investment: the five of us have been willing to invest, but at a level that's been unacceptable to the entrepreneur in front of us.

The equity equation

Angels ask for a meaningful equity stake in new businesses for three reasons. Firstly, it represents the size of the risk they are taking by putting in tens of thousands of pounds (*of their own money*) without asking for any security in return. Secondly, angels often get involved at a fairly early stage of a business, and this makes their investment all the riskier. Thirdly, angels know that with them on board, the venture is far more likely to succeed, so the relatively high percentage also represents the value they add to a company.

I honestly believe that first-time entrepreneurs should not be too concerned about the percentage they give away to attract investment (bar a few exceptions that I'll come to shortly). I completely understand that you don't want a stranger muscling in on your idea – your baby – but being stingy with the equity you give away can actually hinder your progress.

I've found that the following illustration can help people become more comfortable with the idea of giving away equity. I'll keep the maths simple: let's say that your company is worth £100 and that you own 100 per cent of it. The value of £100 represents your idea, your time and your effort (what's sometimes called 'sweat equity' because you had to work so hard to get it). You approach an angel for an investment of £80, which, if you get it, would give your business a new valuation of £180 (your sweat equity plus the cash), and in exchange the angel seeks 40 per cent of your business. This would mean your 60 per cent is worth £108, which is more than the value of your company without the angel's investment. So you can own 100 per cent of a £100 company and forfeit the investment, or you can own 60 per cent of a £180 company and get not just an angel's money, but their experience and expertise too.

Jeff Bezos, the founder of Amazon.com, owns less than 25 per cent of the company he started at the beginning of the dotcom boom. He gave away equity in Amazon at several different rounds of investment so that he could grow his business. He now owns a quarter of a multi-billion-dollar company, rather than 100 per cent of something everyone's forgotten about.

I sometimes think about what might have happened to the people behind Baby Dream Machine if they had been prepared to negotiate on equity. They were the very first people to appear on *Dragons' Den*, and several of us were prepared to invest in their invention that rocked babies to sleep. They thought we wanted too much equity and left the Den with nothing. They came back in the second series, and although there were lots of reasons why they left without investment for a second time, the major reason was that in the intervening year a rival was launched. Baby Dream Machine missed its moment, and now the founders own a large chunk of not very much, rather than a slightly smaller chunk of an internationally successful business.

There's another reason why I think giving away equity to a good angel is a smart way to proceed, especially if this is your first business: you will learn things in weeks that might otherwise take you years. The right angel can accelerate your business (let's face it, they want to get their money back as soon as they can) so that instead of building a multi-million-pound business in a decade, you can do it in two or three years. At the end of those two or three years, you will be worth millions yourself and you'll be highly skilled and extremely well placed to do it all over again. Only this time you can fund the venture yourself and keep 100 per cent of it.

That said, I do have one word of warning about giving away too much equity too soon. By now, you should have an idea of the sort of company you want to build, and if you think that at some point you might want to bring in a second round of investment, then you need to be a little careful. Second rounds of investment – typically from venture capitalists or stock-market flotation – often need to raise millions of pounds, usually to fund a big hike in advertising or production or both. If you've already given away a large piece of your company, to raise those extra millions you might have to offer an even bigger piece of your pie to secondary investors. But, like Jeff Bezos, if you're only left with a minority percentage, it doesn't much matter if the company's worth millions.

Approaching an angel

At the end of this chapter is a list of websites where you can find links to several angel investors. You should spend some time going through the list and searching the internet for the names of others. Your local chamber of commerce will also be able to put you in touch with local investors, as will your local branch of Business Link.

As you search, you should be keeping an eye out for an investor who is a good match for your business. Ideally, it will be someone who has worked in your industry and who has contacts and sector knowledge that can accelerate your progress. You also want to think about the kind of angel you want at your shoulder. Do you want someone who will take over and sit in the driving seat? Or do you want someone who can act as more of a mentor?

When you have identified four or five angels who you would like to be a part your business, approach them – or sometimes their PA – and say how much you admire them (flattery never goes amiss, although syco-phancy could see you filed in the bin) and that you'd like to approach them with an investment opportunity. Some investors have their own websites that will tell you how to submit a proposal, but if not, ask how they would like to receive the information. By email? In the post? And would they like the whole plan or just the executive summary? After the initial contact, send the material as soon as possible with a covering letter introducing yourself and your business. If it is appropriate and logistically possible, send them a sample of your product.

You should at least get an acknowledgement that they've received it within a week, and if you haven't had a reply after a month, then I think it is acceptable to get back in touch and politely remind them that you are speaking to other investors, but that you really would prefer to work with them.

The next step will either be a request for further information or an invitation to go and meet them. Of course, you might get a rejection. You shouldn't automatically assume that this means your business isn't any good – just look at *Dragons' Den*, where each week one of us invests in something the others are not interested in. There could be any number of reasons why the investor turns you down. It could just be that they are too busy to take on another project.

Making your pitch

If you've seen *Dragons' Den*, then you have some idea of what happens at a pitch meeting between an entrepreneur and an investor. Whether or not it's as formal as standing up next to a flip chart or running through a PowerPoint presentation will vary from investor to investor (there's no harm in asking in advance whether they are expecting a formal presentation). But one way or another, after the handshakes, you will be expected to present your business opportunity.

If you are part of a launch team, I would advise you not to take the entire team with you – just the person in charge and the person who deals with the money. If that's the same person, then one person should be sufficient. However, the entire team should have a hand in developing and refining the pitch and must completely support the person sent to do the job. It's a difficult job, and knowing there are doubters back at the office makes it that bit harder.

If possible, you should demonstrate what your company does: if you have a product, take it; if you offer a service, show a video of your service being carried out to demonstrate the benefit to your customers. You should also take a copy of your business plan (just in case the investor has someone else in the room who needs to read it too), and copies of any relevant supporting paperwork, such as order confirmations and patent certificates.

Standing up and giving presentations is something that most people find hard, but after several years of *Dragons' Den*, I have noticed that the people who perform best are those who are most convinced of their business case. I therefore suggest that whatever doubts you have about giving a presentation can be partially allayed by resolving any doubts you have about your business. If you're not entirely confident about your financial forecast, or where your next ten customers are coming from, then I'll bet you'll find pitching a lot harder. Let me put it this way: like all selling, if you really believe that you can make your investor a fortune, then there is a far greater chance that he or she will believe it too.

You don't need to prepare a PowerPoint presentation (unless it has been asked for), but preparing one can act as a prompt to stop you from drying up mid-flow. I would suggest that five or six slides, each tackling a different aspect of your business – the idea, the market, the team, the finance and the opportunity (i.e. how much you want and the amount of equity you're offering in return) – broken down into bullet points. What you don't want to do is read through your business plan.

When you've finished your presentation, be prepared for a serious grilling. Expect to be asked about every aspect of your business and to articulate exactly how you will use the investment. The sorts of things investors like you to do with their money are to increase production, or marketing, or to exploit a new market. What we never want to hear is that you are going to use our money to pay yourself a nice little salary. It's not that we don't want you to be able to pay your mortgage, but history is full of new companies where investment has been swallowed up in a matter of months by salary costs. And besides, if you're not being paid adequately, you'll stay hungry for success. Getting investment isn't the end of your journey, it's just a bloody big milestone along the way.

This meeting is also a chance for you to ask questions. You should find out what the investor is offering in addition to their cash. Are they prepared to be your mentor? Your chairman? Can they make introductions for you? Make sure you understand exactly what they are offering – can you call them up day and night, or do they just want to see your annual accounts?

Beyond that, I have four rules that anyone pitching to me should always follow. I imagine most investors will want to hear the same things.

1 Give me a pitch I understand. Don't over-complicate things, don't blind me with science or make me feel stupid because I haven't heard of a new craze or piece of technology. Simply tell me what you do, why

you do it, why your idea is better than your competitors', how your customers will know you exist and why you're the right person to lead the company.

2 Be honest and open. Give me simple, straightforward answers to my questions. Don't make impossible promises and indulge in pie-in-the-sky talk – even if you think you're being honest, there's a chance you'll come across as implausible. If you don't know the answer to something, come clean.

3 Know your numbers. If you don't know how much your offering costs to produce, or what you can charge for it, or its profit margin, then you're not going to impress anyone. You should have all sorts of figures on the tip of your tongue, not at your fingertips. You should know how many competitors you have, what my return on capital will be and exactly how you will spend my money. If you don't know your numbers, it can come across that you're trying to hide something and you'll appear deceitful.

4 Tell me the exit strategy. I'd love to see you become a success, but more than that, I want to make money, so don't forget why I'm interested: I want an investment to give me at least a 25 per cent return within a couple of years. You need to tell me how much money I can expect to make and how and when I can expect to get my cash out.

What happens next?

Unlike the Den, where contestants leave with an offer of a deal, in the real world, most investors will usually get back to you a few days later with their assessment. They might want to make background checks into your business or your market before they make you an offer. They might want to discuss it with colleagues. They might just not like making quick decisions. If you aren't offered a deal there and then, make sure to ask when you can expect to have heard from them by – after all, you're speaking to lots of other investors too.

An angel *might* then come back to you and say, 'I'll give you all the money you want for the percentage you're offering,' but that's very unlikely. The chances are that they will want to cut some kind of deal. Some of the things that might come up are:

Match funding

This is where an investor will give you some of the money if you get the rest of it from other sources. This might not be what you want to hear, but it's very good news: it will be much easier to persuade another investor if you've already got one committed.

A non-dilution clause

This means that if an angel takes a stake in your company, that stake cannot be diluted by second or third rounds of fundraising.

Dividend policy

The circumstances when dividends will become payable are set out in advance. Some investors want income as well as capital growth and may insist on payment from profits in the short term rather than waiting for an exit strategy to realise their investment in the long term. The rates of pay-outs are also occasionally negotiated at this time, e.g. when profits hit £100,000 a dividend of x per cent will be paid.

Drag and tag

This clause ensures that the investor is entitled to the same share allowances as the founder. This allows the investor to protect the size of their stake and prevents the founder, who is usually the majority shareholder, from benefiting from a sale of stock without the investor also benefiting. If the majority shareholder increases their shareholding, the investor *drags* along and increases their holding by the same percentage. If the

majority shareholder sells their shares, the investor *tags* along
and their shares must be sold at the same time.

Even if you are offered the full amount, it's likely that the angel will ask
for more equity than you want to give away. You don't have to accept the
offer and are expected to negotiate. If someone doesn't negotiate with
me, I begin to wonder if they are likely to negotiate the best deals with
suppliers and customers. Once you have come to a figure, you don't have
to accept it there and then. Just as investors can take a day or two to make
you an offer, you can take a bit of time to decide whether or not to accept
it. Not only might you want to discuss it with your mentor, partner and colleagues, but you might also be waiting to hear from another investor. If
you are offering a genuine chance to make money, then you can expect
to be the subject of a bidding war. There is no better negotiation tool for
lowering the percentage you have to give away than having two offers on
the table.

The percentage isn't the only thing you should consider when you're
making your decision. Different investors have different attributes, and
one who can give you the support you need might be worth giving away
a bit more equity for. I would like to be able to say that these discussions
should be a negotiation between equals but, in reality, it's rarely the case.
Yes, you're offering to make the investor a big return, but only the most
arrogant first-timer would fail to see that the investor has the upper hand.
These deals are unbalanced for a couple of reasons: firstly, the entrepreneur may be unused to negotiations, while the investor does it every day;
secondly, the law of supply and demand means that the investor could
put their money somewhere else, whereas the entrepreneur has a pretty
limited supply of money sources.

You might be frustrated by the imbalance in your negotiating position,
but having been involved in a lot of these negotiations, I can honestly
say that the best deal is the one that enables you to get on with business
and propel your company forward. Maybe if you waited a month or two

you might get a better deal, percentage-wise, but you might have missed out on countless opportunities in the meantime, not to mention the momentum and enthusiasm that can be lost in that time. If you get a good enough offer, take it.

Once you have accepted an offer, you will then enter into a process known as 'due diligence', and this is where a lot of deals fall apart. Your investor will ask for proof that everything you've told them about the investment opportunity is true. You will need to show your Articles of Association (if you are a limited company), any patent documentation, your accounts and any written confirmation of anything crucial to the investment – like deals with suppliers and clients.

This can be a rigorous and time-consuming process, and it may throw up some problems. The investor may have assumed the investment was in the *company*, whereas you might have thought you had made it clear you were offering a stake in the *product*. All these issues will be ironed out through due diligence, and if they are concluded to both parties' satisfaction, then you can expect a large amount of money to be transferred to your account!

Pros and cons of business angels

Pros	Cons
You get help as well as cash	Some have been known to take over
You gain credibility for having someone experienced on the team	You might have to give away more equity than you'd hoped
Unlike a loan, there are no repayments to make out of cashflow	The process can take a long time

---

Angel resources

British Business Angels Association www.bbaa.org.uk
This is the recognised hub for people wanting to invest and get investment in new businesses in the UK.

Angels Den (can't think where they got the name from!) www.angelsden.com
A relatively new venture, Angels Den aims to put businesses and investors in touch with each other as easily and quickly as possible.

UK Business Incubation www.ukbi.co.uk
Incubation is a slightly more hands-on form of angel investment where you get day-to-day help as well as investment.

Brainspark plc www.brainspark.com
This is one of the few dotcom investors to have survived, so they must be getting something right!

● ● ● ● ● **BANNATYNE'S BOOTCAMP** ● ● ● ● ●

Negotiating

I've read lots of business books over the years that spout on about techniques for negotiating, and I have to say almost all of them are rubbish. I don't know if there really are people out there who think it will make a big difference if they sit with their back to the window (so that their 'opponent' will be forced to squint into the sunlight and won't be able to see their facial expressions), but if there are, then they are taking life far too seriously. Negotiations almost always happen between two parties who both stand to gain from the outcome: there just aren't that many win-lose negotiations to be had. That doesn't mean you shouldn't always try to get the price you want, but I find saying things like 'Help me out here. If you can do it for twenty per cent less, I can give you the business' works much better than outright demands.

You rarely have to agree to a deal there and then, and stalling can be an effective tool. People might say, 'If you agree to this today, you can have it for this price,' but in reality if they can offer a good price today, they'll be able to offer it next week. So say to them, 'That's a good price. If I don't get a better offer, I'll be back in touch.'

I like to keep my options open, so I tend to keep negotiations going for as long as possible and occasionally to say yes to things just to see what happens if we keep talking. On any important negotiation, there will be contracts involved and the finer details can usually be ironed out further down the line.

There are four aspects of negotiations that I think are the most important:

1   A deal that allows you to get on with your business is probably better than a cheaper deal that takes time to pull together. You can always renegotiate later on to get a better price.

2   Know your bottom line. If there's a price you won't go above, or below, stick to your guns. Don't blow your budget just to save face.

3   Don't say any more than you have to. Giving away information can be like giving away ammunition.

4   You can walk away. There will almost always be another deal out there if you don't like what's on the table.

● ●

Venture capitalists

A venture capitalist firm is typically a large organisation that invests its clients' money in new businesses with the hope of producing spectacular profits. These are big City institutions with millions to play with, and they are all on the lookout for the Next Big Thing.

Dealing with a VC isn't that different from getting investment from an angel: you send them your business plan; if they like it, you will be asked to make a presentation; if you get through due diligence, you will get investment. However, there are some very big differences between VC money and angel money.

The obvious difference is that VCs have more money, and their level of investment usually starts where angel investment stops. If you need more than £250,000, you will either need to raise it from a variety of sources or you will need to find VC investment. For me, the biggest difference between angels and VCs is that instead of dealing with a fellow entrepreneur, you find yourself talking to an employee.

In my experience, the sort of people who go to work for venture capitalists are university graduates who often delay their immersion in the real world by subsequently studying for an MBA. They thrive in a corporate world, not the commercial world, and are personally motivated by annual bonuses and promotions. They are basically bank managers with a slightly more enlightened attitude to risk. Understanding – and accepting – the culture clash between entrepreneurs and the kinds of people who typically work for big City firms is the key to getting what you want out of them.

Institutional investors play a numbers game. Doug Richard of Library House once told me that VCs expect nine out of ten ventures to fail because they invest in such high-risk projects. They therefore need to find the one-in-ten companies that make up those losses and deliver spectacular rewards. This is not the place to take an investment that offers a 25 per cent return: they want 200 per cent – at least. In order to give themselves the best possible chance of the best possible returns, VCs will sometimes make very serious demands on the companies they invest in. That may include imposing a chairman on you, or a financial director, or an intrusive monitoring method.

There's a reason for this: when a VC puts money in, they are usually looking at taking your company to a stock-market flotation at the earliest opportunity, and so they start grooming your company to look attractive to the markets. They can install non-executive board members (often on a substantial salary for just a few hours' work), suggest you get your accounts done by one of the leading international accountancy firms, and employ a PR agency whose sole job it is to get future investors interested in your company.

Within weeks, your start-up venture can be turned into something that feels more like a multinational, and if that happens, you need extraordinary strength of mind to focus on what really matters. It can be incredibly exciting, but it can also be nerve-wracking. However, with so much expertise around you, it's possible to grow your company spectacularly quickly, and if you hold on tight, you could be in for the ride of your life!

> **6** *Understanding the culture clash between entrepreneurs and big City firms is the key to getting what you want out of them.* **9**

Venture capital resources

The British Private Equity and Venture Capital Association
www.bvca.co.uk
This is the umbrella organisation for venture capitalists in the UK.

3i www.3i.com
This is one of the biggest venture capital firms in the country. Their website gives insights into what they expect from their investments.

Apax Partners www.apax.com
This is another of the really big players. Look at their website to find out about their investment criteria.

IIIIIIIIIIIIIIIIIIIIIIIIIIIIIIIII **CASE STUDY** IIIIIIIIIIIIIIIIIIIIIIIIIIIIIII

Name: Eugenie Harvey **Age**: 39
Job: Social entrepreneur; director of We Are What We Do
Qualifications: BA in communications from University of
Technology, Sydney
www.wearewhatwedo.org

My background is in corporate communications in Australia, working
for big organisations like Rupert Murdoch's Foxtel. I had a good job, I
was pretty good at it, a nice salary, but it really didn't make me happy.
I'd always had the idea that I wanted to do something that made the
world a better place, but if I'm honest, I always found that a slightly
embarrassing ambition. As I approached 30, I really wasn't sure which
way to go, so I decided to make use of the fact that I have a British
passport and came to the UK. I thought that I could start again in
England where I would have the freedom to fail if I tried something
new. However, straight away I found myself working back in PR.
Although the work was good, I was becoming increasingly depressed
with corporate life and I started looking around to see if there was
something else I could do.

When you truly commit to a course of action, I think fate has a funny
way of stepping in and helping you find your way. I was working for
a financial PR firm called Brunswick, when they invited the founder
of a local charity to come and talk to the staff about his work. His
name was David Robinson and his charity, Community Links (www.
community-links.org), runs projects in Canning Town in East London.
David is very charismatic and inspirational, and at the end of the
session I asked to find out more about his work. He invited me out to
Canning Town to visit some of their projects, and a couple of months
later he handed me a paper he'd written about how people of my
generation were falling away from community involvement. In the
1980s, something like 60 per cent of people in their thirties were

members of, or regularly participated in, some kind of community organisation, but that figure has dropped to around 6 per cent. We started to discuss ways in which people could be encouraged to re-engage, and this started one of the most rewarding periods of my career. I spent the next two years talking to people and refining a very loose proposition into something tangible.

David invited a group of business leaders, creative specialists and government insiders to come together to discuss these ideas further, and I could see there was a lot of interest from some potentially very influential people. I thought there might be a role for me project-managing their ideas and seeing if I could make them something manifest.

I had been saving up a deposit to buy a flat, but I decided instead to quit my job in November 2002 and use that money to live on. I was 33; I didn't have any of the commitments I'd expected to have at that age and realised that I had this enormous amount of freedom to take a risk. I was very lucky in that I was able to house-sit for friends, so I could live quite modestly for a while, and that kept me going until we received a grant from the Joffe Charitable Trust, which allowed me to keep developing the ideas until we launched. People tell me I must have been terribly brave to give up my job, but the truth is, I was so miserable that I honestly didn't feel like I had much of a choice.

The project developed into We Are What We Do and our challenge was to take a very basic idea – that a simple action done by a million people can change the world – and make a difference. We knew that books like *The Little Book of Calm* had sold millions of copies, so we decided to create a book of simple actions that people could do to help with big problems – like poverty, climate change and crime – that together would make a big difference. Things like turning the tap off when you brush your teeth.

We knew the book's content had to be compelling, and crucially it had to be cool, and so we enlisted the help of fantastic designers, illustrators and photographers – who all volunteered their time and talent – and we produced *Change the World for a Fiver*. Rebecca Nicolson had just started her publishing house Short Books and agreed to publish the book without making any money out of it. She introduced us to Random House, who agreed to do the distribution for free. It is amazing how people will respond to you when you approach them with passion and commitment.

Our books are not cheap to produce – they contain stickers and fold-out sections and loads of other gimmicks – but I was determined that they had to retail for £5 as they had to be accessible and not elitist. However, when we did our original calculations we didn't know to factor in the commission that retailers take. Rebecca called me up in a bit of a panic a couple of weeks before we went to press: with the retailers' commission, a book called *Change the World for a Fiver* was going to have to retail at £6.40!

Somehow, and I can't even think how this happened now, but I had struck up a good relationship with the buyer at Waterstones and so I called her up and said, 'You've got to help us.' She agreed to take 5000 copies at just a 10 per cent commission, and that meant we were in business.

David had been working with the then chancellor Gordon Brown for some time, and he kindly agreed to host a breakfast book launch for us at Downing Street that we invited business leaders to. He told everyone there what a great project we had and that people should do what they could to help. Within 20 minutes, we had orders for another 35,000 copies – 28,000 of them from Sainsbury's. To cut a long story short, *Change the World for a Fiver* sold 100,000 copies in 100 days and I suddenly found myself at the centre of a media storm. It's been full steam ahead ever since, and we've now had several successful projects that are starting to raise awareness and make a difference. We published a second title in 2006, *Change the World 9 to 5*, and we are now on the verge of selling our millionth book. We also had amazing success with our 'I'm Not a Plastic Bag' campaign when a bag we produced with Anya Hindmarch became a must-have fashion accessory.

That's making it sound a bit too straightforward, as the truth was much harder. The publishing industry insisted on reverting to normal terms after our 100,000th sale, so we are now in the difficult position where we make a loss every time we sell a book through a shop. We keep costs to a minimum: my old boss, Alan Parker, at Brunswick Public Relations, kindly gives us free office space and we are reliant on volunteers for some of our work.

Although I had some financial-management skills from my previous career, I have had to learn so much in the past few years – I went from producing a book to running a fast-moving small business in the space of three years. Perhaps the biggest challenge was a problem most new businesses would love to have: how to deal with being successful! Success brings its own challenges and managing the force we unleashed hasn't always been easy – we didn't even have the cash to print more copies of the book in the early days!

One of the things I'm working hard at now is making sure our transition from a handful of volunteers to a team of professionals doesn't mean we lose the spirit that has got us so far so quickly. Our challenge is to take what we've achieved and build on it to turn We Are What We Do into a global force. I didn't start We Are What We Do to make a million: I was clear that I wanted to make a difference, and I see rewarding work and a decent salary as my exit strategy.

What's the best advice you've ever had? Someone said to me recently, 'You're a start-up, just remember that,' and this has become very important to me. Coming from a corporate, well-funded background,

I worry that my staff don't always have the best working conditions and we don't always do things as well as I might like, or know exactly what is the best decision for us to take in a situation we've never been in before. It was important to be reminded that working for a start-up isn't like that: just because it's chaotic and cashflow is still an issue, that doesn't mean we've failed. That's just what it's like for most new businesses.

What do you wish you'd known from the start? I suppose it would have been nice to have had some idea that we would have been so successful so quickly, because then we could have planned for it a bit better. But I wonder if we'd had that knowledge if we'd have been so tenacious. And perhaps it wouldn't have been as exciting.

What's the one thing you'd say to someone starting their first business? If you really believe in something, then you really must go for it. You cannot fail to find a sense of fulfilment. It takes a bit of courage, but it's worth it.

IIIIIIIIIIIIIIIIIIIIIIIIIIIIIIIIIIIIIIIIIIIIIIIIIIIIIIIIIIIIIIIIIIIIIIIIIIIIIIIIIIIIIIII

6 Running your business

In this chapter, I'd like to run through the practical aspects of getting a company off the ground and managing its day-to-day affairs – things like hiring staff, filling in VAT returns and finding premises. These are simple things, but I know from talking to a lot of new entrepreneurs that the fear of 'red tape' and bookkeeping is very real. However, after 30 years in business, I can promise you that practically everything to do with running a business comes down to just one thing – common sense.

I've come to realise that managing a business is what I'm really good at and it's actually where I make the most difference. There are several health-club operators, but I bet I run my business more efficiently than any of my competitors. Looking back, I can see it was my willingness and ability to take charge of my care-home business that made it such a success. Good management can make a good company great.

If this is your first business and your previous career hasn't exposed you to any of the language or processes of management, I understand that it can be daunting. But as I said right at the beginning of this book, one of the things that singles entrepreneurs out for success is their ability to take responsibility for their companies. And that's what this chapter is all about: taking responsibility.

Firstly, I'd like to share a bit of information I discovered early on in my career. It's not particularly exciting, or revelatory, but it is very helpful: no matter what you do in business, I can promise you one thing – there is a leaflet that makes it easier. Whether it's your health and safety obligations, registering for VAT or calculating your employer's National Insurance contributions, the government has produced a leaflet on it and won't charge a penny to send it to you. They're all available to download from various government websites, and if you take the time to read them rather than shoving your fingers in your ears, shutting your eyes and screaming, 'Blah, blah, blah' (which I know is a lot of people's first response), you'll actually find them very helpful. And not only will you save yourself a fortune in professional fees, but you will also learn about business in general, and get to know your own business intimately. Take my advice: take responsibility for the small stuff, and the big stuff will come much more easily.

Don't forget, as I've said before, you're not expected to know everything straight away. The chances are, you may never need to know the difference between something being exempt from VAT and it being zero-rated for VAT, so don't worry too much about irrelevant details. As your business grows, your knowledge about business will grow naturally, so don't look on this as some big operational headache. It's all just common sense.

❝ Good management can make a good company great: take responsibility for the small stuff, and the big stuff will come much more easily. ❞

What's in a name?

Getting your company, product and brand name right can take a surprising amount of time. The industry you're in might govern your choice – you might buy a children's puzzle called Whacko, but you wouldn't use an accountancy firm with that name – but your company name is generally something you have a free rein over.

A company name conveys certain things about your operation to the outside world, and this means there might be more to consider than you first thought. Take a moment to think about existing company names you like, and try to work out why you respond to them. As you work out what suits your company best, here are some things you might like to consider.

What should your name say about you?

Do you want to seem young and vibrant, or is it important for you to appear sober and traditional? If you're opening a sandwich shop, do you want to be Jill's Sandwich Shop, the slightly racier Jill's Baps, the direct Fast & Tasty or the upmarket Egg & Cress? Each of these names is capable of getting the punters in, and it's not difficult to see that each name conveys slightly different things to potential customers.

Ask yourself if it's important that your company name says what the company actually does, e.g. Brown's Financial Management, or Brown's Estate Agency, or can you just be Brown's? Remember, people won't only be looking for you on the high street, they'll be calling up directory enquiries and asking for an estate agent, or searching online for one. They're unlikely to put Brown's into Google if they want to find a particular trade, so sometimes the boring option can be the most profitable: Brown's Building Supplies is going to find a lot more customers than Brown's Acme Trading.

Who is your market?

Let's stick with sandwich shops for a minute. If you're opening up opposite a factory where there are a lot of workers wanting a quick lunch, any of the first three names would get you some business, whereas the last one would perhaps just get you some stick. However, if you're hoping to appeal to the Yummy Mummy lunchtime trade, then Egg & Cress would probably create the right image. Make sure your company name means something to your potential customers. If you want teenagers to like you, you don't want to call yourself something dull and unpronounceable.

Is the domain name available?

These days, most businesses have a website and it's ideal if your web address – your domain name – is the same as your company name. As you come up with company names, check out the matching domain availability at a site such as www.lowcostdomains.com. Unless you have a particularly unusual name, you'll probably find that the domain you want is already taken. Ideally, you want as short and as memorable a domain name as possible and, depending on your business, it may be worth coming up with a domain name first and letting that decide your company name. If you really can't find your domain, try adding 'online' or 'UK' to the end of it, or start it with an 'i' for internet or 'e' for electronic. If at all possible, you want to be a .com, and if that's not available, then a .co.uk. You should avoid the strange, unmemorable and unprofessional suffixes like .me.uk and .ltd.uk.

Of course, it goes without saying that if someone is using the domain you want, you should check out their website. Surfers often get confused about suffixes and will go to widgets.com before visiting your site at widgets.co.uk. If widgets.com is a rival, then you may have just lost a sale, and if it's a porn site, then people might assume that you are the pornographer! If either of these are the case, you may want to go back to the drawing board and come up with a completely different name.

Is anyone else using it?

It's pretty obvious why you don't want to use a name that someone else already trades under. Not only is it confusing for customers, but the existing trader may try to sue you for what's known as 'passing off'. There are some pretty simple ways you can check if the name you want is already in use.

* Call directory enquiries and ask for the name you want to use. If they don't have a listing for a company by that name, then you might be in luck.

* Visit www.companieshouse.gov.uk, where you'll find a searchable list of every limited company in the UK. Simply type in your chosen name, and if the search doesn't come up with an exact match, then bingo!

* Go to the Intellectual Property Office's website at www.ipo.gov.uk where they have a searchable list of every active trademark in the UK. If someone has already trademarked the name you want to use, it could cause confusion and you may not be allowed to use it.

Try it out

When you've been struggling with several different names for a long time, it's easy to lose perspective. You can become quite fond of a name you thought of early on, and it can blind you to better suggestions that come along later. Whether you can't decide, or whether you're absolutely sure of what to call your business, there's no harm in trying it out.

Ask friends and family for their opinion. If you're opening a shop, stop people in the street you intend to trade in and ask them which name they prefer. Run the names by as many people who are likely to be future customers as you can and see which one they respond to best.

When I registered my care-homes business with Companies House, I couldn't believe that the name I wanted was still available. Quality Care Homes Ltd seemed such an obvious choice as it conveyed that we offered a better service than anyone else, and I think when you choose a word like quality you feel a responsibility to live up to the expectations attached to it. I had far more difficulty coming up with a name for my first health club: it was quite hard to think of something distinctive or that would mean something to potential members. It was my wife who suggested calling it Bannatyne's. A few gyms nearby had been badly run and members had lost money. By then, I was well known locally as a responsible business-man and putting my name to the club meant potential members would know their money and banking details were being handled by someone they could trust.

Logos and branding

While you're giving some thought as to how your company name com-municates certain things about you to potential clients and customers, it's worth talking about how your logo and branding influences their choices too. This may not be something you need to worry too much about if you're buying and selling on eBay, but if you'll be having a direct trading relationship with your customers, then it's important to get it right.

It's amazing how influenced we are by branding. I'm not talking about mega brands like Nike and Prada, but how the everyday packaging of products and services guides the decisions we make. We choose lawyers that have sober names (Lawrence & Marks, rather than We Get You Off) engraved on simple brass plaques by their front door, but if we were booking a party organiser, we'd want someone who tied balloons to their front door and called themselves something exciting like PartyTime! rather than Tina's Events Services. Whether it's balloons or brass plaques, the way you present yourself is crucial.

Some companies' success is entirely down to the brand. The painkiller Nurofen, for example, contains exactly the same amount of the key ingre-dient – ibuprofen – as chemists' own-brand painkillers, yet it is a market leader even though it is twice as expensive. Take pop bands: often the music is very mediocre, but their fans buy it because they respond to the overall package of dancing, fashion, smiles and clear skin. Two identical products can launch at the same time to the same market with the same price, but the one that gets their brand right will put the other out of business.

I'm not a brand expert, and if you think your business will live or die by its branding, then you will probably need a dedicated branding book and possibly the services of a professional branding agency. However, I've learnt enough over the years to realise that branding is basically about conveying your values to your customers. You might want to indicate that your product or service is honest, fun, upmarket, ethical or fast. Values are not always easy to pin down and they can be quite abstract, but once you've worked out what they are, then it becomes easier to establish a brand that means something to your customers. The best way I know to do this is to come up with three words – just three words – that you want your customers to associate with your company. Perhaps it would help if I gave you a few examples.

* Virgin – fun, anti-establishment, good value

* Nationwide Building Society – trustworthy, customer-focused, friendly

* Marks & Spencer – quality, value, customer service

* Bannatyne Health Clubs – friendly, dynamic, quality

Once you have come up with the three words that sum up your offering, you need to ask yourself if you're conveying these things effectively. Is your headed notepaper, your website design or your shop front telling customers what you stand for as well as what you do? Do each of the ways you communicate with your customers say the same thing? If you have a shabby website but a swanky product, you will be sending conflicting messages to the public. As a new business, the best way to establish your business with your customers is to give them a consistent 'message', and each way you communicate with them should give the same message.

There are a number of design agencies that can help you design a logo and advise on the colours you can use to convey the right message. You can keep their price down by having a clear idea of what you want and briefing them thoroughly. No designer wants to hear, 'Do whatever you think is best.' What they want is clear instruction: 'Here's a selection of logos I like from other companies; our brand values are fun, impulsiveness and speed; I want the main colour to be red.'

Getting artwork done is much cheaper than it used to be. There are dedicated design companies online such as www.britishlogos.co.uk that will come up with a choice of logos for under £100. A Google search will come up with several more. However, you might be able to do it for free, as most computers these days are sold with a bundle of software that will enable someone with a bit of talent to do it themselves. Teenagers can be handy for this sort of thing, as not only are they technically more proficient than most adults, but they always seem to have a friend who can build a website, design a flyer or rustle up a logo.

Brands aren't static: if your business changes, your brand and logo may need to change too. In my organisation, we realised that the name Bannatyne had become a brand when my profile was raised by *Dragons' Den*, and that meant making a few changes. For instance, my hotel in Darlington – which had previously been called the Grange – became Hotel Bannatyne. It made sense to have the same logo across all my companies – health clubs, bars, property development, hotels – but the logo we used for the health clubs was a bit too sporty for an upmarket hotel, so we had a classier logo designed. This is now being used on all my new Bannatyne ventures.

Branding isn't crucial to all companies, and it may well be the case that this isn't something that should be taking up too much of your time and budget at an early stage. It can also be the case that 're-branding' later in your development can provide you with an opportunity for a bit of coverage in the media. Only you can decide if this is something you need to concentrate on, or if it is a distraction from getting closer to your goal.

Sole trader, partnership or limited company?

Choosing the right legal structure for the ownership of your company is something that I know concerns a lot of first-time entrepreneurs. Many think becoming a limited company will make them look respectable, but don't understand the processes and commitments involved.

Sole trader

This is the easiest and cheapest way of trading if you are setting up a business from home that won't be employing staff for the foreseeable future. It's how I ran my ice-cream business because it's no different from being self-employed, which means it doesn't require any ongoing paperwork. Within three months of starting your business, however, you have a duty to inform the Inland Revenue of your self-employed status. You can download the necessary form at www.inlandrevenue.gov.uk.

Your income from your business will be treated alongside any other moonlighting income and many of your expenses will become deductible against tax. You will need to complete an annual Self-Assessment Tax Return and pay tax on your profits. You will also need to pay National Insurance contributions on your profits as well as Class 2 NI contributions of £2.30 a week (for 2008/09). If your business makes a loss, you can offset this against any other earnings you might have elsewhere.

You will need to keep good records of your expenses and your income, and as long as you do this, handling your own tax affairs shouldn't be too difficult. If completing your tax return is something you find daunting, a local accountant should prepare your accounts for a modest fee (£200 is a reasonable ballpark figure if your needs are straightforward). You'll see from many of the case studies in this book that other entrepreneurs are happy to outsource their accountancy. If you know that getting to grips with your paperwork is a bad use of your time and your expertise, then get a recommendation for a good accountant. Just make sure that you don't see the accounts as someone else's responsibility: they're your accounts, and you should always be on top of the headline figures.

Self-employed people pay their tax in annual or six-monthly instalments. This means you will get into difficulty when your tax bill becomes due if you haven't set aside your tax. The good news is that you can earn interest on it for over a year before you have to hand it over.

You can cease being a sole trader whenever you want to, which means when your company grows and you want to formalise its status, there's no tedious 'winding-up' paperwork to deal with. In my view, this is the ideal way for a very young, very small business; however, if you want to raise investment, few backers will put money into a venture without a legal ownership status.

Pros and cons of being a sole trader

Pros	Cons
Easy, cheap and flexible	Unlimited liability for any company
Low NI costs	debts
Few statutory controls	May hinder fundraising

Partnership

If you're starting a business with friends, then setting up as a partnership is an option you should consider. Partnerships are very similar, legally, to sole traders in that you don't need to register your company or prepare any onerous paperwork for anyone outside the company. All you need to do is draw up an agreement between the partners. There are a few sorts of partnership, all with slightly different rules, to fit slightly different situations. The reason for this is that partnerships can be unstable – one partner leaves, or spends less time than promised on the venture – and so partnership agreements are about making sure the partners honour their commitments to each other.

One of the key drawbacks of working in a partnership is that all partners become equally responsible for the debt of the company. So if one of you takes out a loan in the company name and scarpers with the cash, you will all be liable for the debt. You may want to consider setting up what's known as a limited liability partnership, where partners' liability is limited to their initial investment. You can find out more at www.companieshouse.gov.uk/infoAndGuide/llp.shtml.

As a partnership, you can still have a company name, but you have a legal requirement to put your own name on any documentation. For instance, your headed notepaper can have your logo and company name, but somewhere in the small print, all the partners' names must be listed. Similarly, if you open up a business account as a partnership, you will probably be issued with cheque books that say, 'Bill Smith and Amy Martin trading as Ace Plumbing,' rather than the straightforward 'Ace Plumbing'.

You will each remain responsible for your own tax affairs, and like sole traders will need to complete an annual Self-Assessment Tax Return. Your share of the profits will be treated like any other form of income. Likewise, your share of the expenses will be deductible against tax.

Although there is no legal requirement to inform the authorities of your partnership, I recommend formalising your arrangement with a partnership agreement; even if you have known your business partner for years. You will need a solicitor to do this, and it sets out who owns what, who gets what share of the profits, and what happens if one party wishes to leave the partnership. It should cost you less than a couple of hundred pounds. I suppose it's a bit like a pre-nuptial agreement: thinking about it isn't nearly as exciting as planning the wedding, but it will save a lot of grief if the partnership ever breaks down. Also, by agreeing roles and responsibilities at the outset, you are much more likely to work constructively with each other.

Limited company

A limited, or limited liability, company is often described as having one big advantage for new businesses: namely that the debts are limited to the amount of shares you own in the company. So, in theory, if you started a company with £100 and it went bust with thousands of pounds worth of debts, all you would owe would be the £100. And if you've already invested that £100, then you would owe nothing. In reality, I think this is pretty spurious, as no new company will be offered credit without the founders offering personal security. The company might be liable for the debt but, in all likelihood, the bank will have asked for your home as security and wouldn't think twice about repossessing it if the company loan defaulted. However, there are other debts that a company might have – to pay VAT, or to pay suppliers or employees – that would be limited to your initial share capital if you went bust. There are also some other advantages to becoming a limited company, but with those advantages come responsibilities, and most of those come in the form of red tape.

A limited company is a separate legal entity that can do things like own property, take out loans, sue other companies and be sued. Because of this, each limited company must have at least one director, who has legal responsibilities for its management. It must also have a company secretary who undertakes to ensure that official records are properly maintained. The director and secretary can be the same person.

Each limited company is registered with Companies House, and no two companies can have the same name. Each year, limited companies must file their accounts, which will be available on a public register.

One of the great advantages of incorporation is that it sets out what each shareholder's stake and responsibilities are. If there are several of you involved in the company, as well as additional investors, then incorporation makes sure your investment in the company is secure.

Setting up a limited company is neither expensive nor time-consuming, and all the information you need is available at www.companieshouse.gov.uk. You can even make your application online. To be eligible, you need three things: a UK address, which will become the company's registered address for official correspondence, a unique company name and £20, which covers the registration fee (you can pay more for an express service).

Companies House staff are trained to help first-timers complete the necessary paperwork, but there are countless firms – usually solicitors or accountants, as well as specialist incorporation firms – who can take on this job for you. I seriously recommend you don't outsource this kind of admin: if you do, there will always be a part of your business you don't understand, and that you will feel is someone else's responsibility.

Not everyone is considered suitable to be a director of a limited company, and if you have a bad credit history, or one of your partners does, then you may be barred. If you have been declared bankrupt, you will usually have to wait until your bankruptcy is discharged before you can apply for a directorship. The benefit of this is that you might find out something about your partners sooner rather than later!

As part of the registration process, you will be asked to produce your Memorandum of Association. This follows a standard template (you can buy blanks in most stationers) and registers the name, the directors and their share capital, your address and the nature of your business. The company address doesn't have to be your home address: if you use an accountant, they will usually let you use theirs. I'd advise you to do this to prevent your home address appearing on the register at Companies House, and therefore being available to marketeers and junk-mail merchants.

Unlike a partnership, where you can simply stop trading if things don't work out, a limited company needs to be officially wound up and any assets distributed proportionally between the shareholders. This can be a

---

Pros and cons of being a limited company

Pros	Cons
It looks respectable	Initial paperwork
Each partner's stake is set out	Ongoing responsibility to
You have limited liability for debts	keep records
	Winding up can take time

---

difficult process at a difficult time if you've gone bust and have enough to deal with elsewhere.

Although there is a lot of paperwork involved and a commitment to file annual accounts, the big benefit of incorporation is that it makes issuing shares to backers or employees (perhaps as part of a share-option scheme) far easier. Limited companies look respectable, and whether you are trying to woo investment or staff, it is generally easier if you are incorporated.

Premises

There are two things that drain the limited resources of new companies like nothing else – staff and premises. If funds are tight, then one of the best ways you can improve cashflow is by not paying any rent. Before you start searching for offices or warehousing space, take a good look at your home and see if you can launch your business from there. I ran my health-club business from my dining table for over a year before I took an office and have never understood entrepreneurs who are in a rush to get an expensive office. I suspect that they only want one because friends and family won't think they've got a 'proper' company until they've got premises.

For a lot of workers these days, their office is a laptop computer and a mobile phone, or even just their BlackBerry. Entire teams of people can now work together remotely using broadband connections and free phone services like Skype. It may be far more cost-effective for you to launch this way and only hire meeting rooms when you need to get together. There are plenty of organisations that offer these facilities – such as Regus and MWB – and they provide state-of-the-art conference and computer facilities. Of course, one of the other benefits of home working is that you do not waste time and money commuting.

If you are worried that giving your home address as your company address looks 'wrong', then you can easily get a PO Box – it costs less than £60 a year. Check out www.royalmail.com for details or ask in your local post office.

This won't work for every new company, and there's no doubt that people enjoy working in an office with great colleagues who generate the feeling that the company is going places. Team spirit is harder to foster and harness when people work apart, and sometimes that spirit, that determination, is what carries a company through a sticky patch. So if your company needs premises, what should you look for?

Firstly, a good price. You need to keep your overheads as low as possible. One way to do this is to share someone else's office. Perhaps an old employer has a few spare desks you can use for a small rent. Or maybe you know some other people looking for an office and could save yourselves some money by renting together.

I ran Quality Care Homes out of a Portakabin in the grounds of my first care home for several years before we moved into a spare room within one of the other homes. It was years before I paid for an HQ. Even today, my offices are far from glamorous.

There are lots of companies that rent out offices with shared bathroom and kitchen facilities. Just look up 'Office Space' in the Yellow Pages to find your closest one. Often their rents are slightly higher per square foot than other providers, but they generally offer more flexible rents, perhaps only requiring one month's notice, rather than six months', which isn't uncommon in the commercial sector. My fellow dragon James Caan's company Avanta designs office suites in such a way that visiting clients would never know the office wasn't your own.

It can be difficult to compare the price of offices, as some include line rental for phones, or maintenance or cleaning, while others charge for these separately. Make sure you know exactly what you are paying for. And just a word of warning: office providers that offer a phone service often reduce the line rental and bump up the call charges. If you and your salespeople are going to be spending a lot of time on the phone, then this can be very costly.

You may not be looking for offices, but a studio or factory where you can produce your product. If your business is likely to be noisy, or smelly, or involve a lot of customers visiting the site, then you need to find premises where the leases and planning consents allow this. Ideally, you don't want to be spending your start-up capital modifying leasehold premises to fit your needs, so seek out properties where your line of work is already being carried out.

If you are looking for commercial premises, it may be best to start off with a stall at a market rather than leasing a shop. Many towns and suburbs have indoor markets where units are let to smaller traders. These are great places to start your retail business as they give you a chance to establish relationships with suppliers and customers before you take on the commitment of higher rents. You might even be able to rent some space within an existing shop, like setting up a shoe concession at the back of a dress shop, or a nail bar within a hair salon.

Of course, there are other expenses that come with having premises. As well as utility bills (and be prepared for these to double if you start working from home), you will need things like public liability insurance that covers you if your customers or staff have an accident and injure themselves. You will also need to abide by health and safety regulations, and these can incur additional costs: it may only be shelling out for some 'no smoking' signs, but it could require alterations for disabled access. You can check your health and safety obligations at www.direct.gov.uk (put 'health and safety' into their search to be taken to the right page).

In the early days of a company, what you need is flexibility, whether that's the ability to rent more space if the company takes off, or to reduce your square footage if you take a tumble. Don't be afraid to negotiate hard to get the terms you want. Landlords might not immediately offer the best deal, but if they want your money, it's surprising how flexible they can become.

Other things to consider when you're looking for premises are:

* Is there enough car parking for customers and staff? Can customers park right outside to load up, or pop in quickly?

* What is access like for deliveries?

* Who are your neighbours? Are they likely to welcome your arrival or make things difficult?

* Will your customers and staff feel safe, especially when it gets dark in winter?

* Are there any planning restrictions that will prevent you putting up your own signage?

* Is there anywhere to get some lunch?

> **6** *There are two things that drain the limited resources of new companies like nothing else – staff and premises.* **9**

Hiring staff

Taking on your first employee is a big step for any new company, but while another pair of hands should free you up to take on other projects and lead the business to new heights, staff also come with something that can trip you up: more red tape. Whether it's insurance or PAYE, as an employer you will have a whole range of new responsibilities.

I know there are lots of new companies that attempt to avoid the red tape by paying for staff on a freelance basis. This certainly has advantages – all the drivers I used in my ice-cream business were self-employed – there's less admin to attend to, but there are regulations that prevent you from employing permanent full-time staff this way. As a new company, you want people pulling together, and if your employees are also working for other companies, they might not always be there when you need them. It's very hard to get team spirit going if you don't have a proper team, so you had better get used to the idea of being an employer.

Insurance

As soon as you have more than one employee, you will need Employer's liability insurance in case a member of staff becomes ill or has an accident at work. Your premiums will vary depending on the number of staff, the size of salaries you pay, your claims history and the risk associated with your sector. You can find a list of authorised insurers from the Financial Services Authority (www.fsa.gov.uk) and additional information from the Health and Safety Executive (www.hse.gov.uk), who enforce compliance. For a small company, insurance should not cost you more than £20 a month.

Taxes

As an employer, you will be responsible for deducting your workers' tax and paying this to the Inland Revenue. You will also have to make sure their National Insurance contributions are deducted, and that your employer's NI contributions (which come on top of the employees' contributions) are made. The Inland Revenue knows this can be daunting, so they produce a very comprehensive New Employer Starter Pack that contains all the literature you will need. You can download it from www.hmrc.gov.uk, or you can call them on 0845 7646 646 and they will post it to you.

As an employer, you have the financial benefit of not having to pay your employees' tax immediately, and you can therefore earn interest on it before you hand it over. If you pay your staff in arrears, this can help your cashflow even more. If you pay your employees on 10 July for their work in June, payments to the Inland Revenue won't have to be made until a month later, on 10 August, and in some businesses this can be an enormous help with cashflow.

If you use an accountant, the chances are that you will be able to get them to handle all your pay roll needs, and depending on the size of your company, this shouldn't cost you more than a couple of hundred pounds a month.

Pensions

The law now requires all companies with more than five employees to provide access to a pension scheme. This can be a private scheme arranged with a broker or insurance company of your choice, but it is more likely to be the new government-sponsored Stakeholder Pension Scheme. You do not need to make contributions, nor are your employees obliged to contribute to it, but if they do, you will be responsible for deducting their contributions and passing them on to the pension provider. A list of registered pension schemes is available from the Pensions Regulator (www.pensionsregulator.gov.uk) and full details about the scheme can be found at www.thepensionservice.gov.uk. In my experience, very few employees are likely to take you up on this service so don't worry too much about it; just keep in mind that it will be something you'll have a legal duty to offer when you take on your fifth employee.

Leave

Employees get ill. Some get pregnant. Full-time employees are also entitled to the statutory minimum of four weeks' paid holiday a year. If you only have a handful of employees and one gets ill, one gets pregnant and the other books a holiday, you could find yourself with a real headache. My own figures at Bannatyne Health Clubs show that PAYE costs rose as our business expanded. I reckoned that for our first year, my salary costs were 108 per cent of what I paid our staff; by year three that figure had risen to 112 per cent to take account of increased leave levels, higher staff turnover and financial settlements when we paid off staff who we asked to leave the company. That means for every £100 I pay my staff, I need to set aside £112 in my staffing budgets. Depending on the nature of your business, the number of parents – and potential parents – you employ and how generous you are with holiday entitlements, maternity and paternity leave, your company's figure could be higher or lower than mine.

Up-to-date information on leave obligations is available from the Department for Business, Enterprise & Regulatory Reform at www.berr.gov.uk. There is also plenty of help on how to meet these obligations from Business

Link (www.businesslink.gov.uk/employment). I don't consider any of these responsibilities particularly onerous, but for young companies where cashflow is tight, having to pay maternity leave *and* the salary for the person you get to cover the absent worker can cut margins to the bone. However, good management can minimise the inconvenience and costs.

● ● ● ● ● **BANNATYNE'S BOOTCAMP** ● ● ● ● ●

Fixed rates

I was once involved in a legal negotiation, at the end of which the other side's legal bill came in at over £1 million. Mine totalled £25,000. This was because I had agreed a fixed fee with my lawyer, and whenever I can I always fix my costs. You should never use professional services on an hourly or daily rate, because jobs will invariably take longer than the initial estimate. And when fees are several hundred pounds an hour, costs can skyrocket in a matter of days.

When I found out that it's standard practice for an architect's fee to be 6 per cent of the build cost, I searched for an architect who would work on a flat fee – I was not going to reward someone if their project overran on timings and costs.

It's not just professional fees I like to fix. All my mortgages are at fixed rates, or on 'cap and collar' deals that limit the impact of interest-rate changes. I'm probably no better off because of these deals, but they have given me security and allowed me to forecast my future profits accurately.

● ●

VAT

The VAT threshold is adjusted every year in the chancellor's Budget. In 2008/09 it was £67,000, and if your turnover is over the threshold, then you are obliged to register for VAT. Many businesses and sole traders with lower turnovers also register voluntarily, as there are financial advantages to doing so. However, there is a catch – you guessed it, a little bit more paperwork.

VAT – value added tax – is levied on most purchases and services in the UK at a flat rate of 17.5 per cent (it's less on fuel and zero on certain other things, like books and children's clothes). If you register for VAT, then you can reclaim the VAT you pay out on all of your purchases, but you must also charge it on all your products and services.

This means that there are some small traders for whom VAT registration is actually a bad idea. By adding 17.5 per cent to their bill they become uncompetitive, particularly if their customers are members of the public who aren't VAT-registered. But for larger companies, where most of their customers are already VAT-registered, then there are real advantages to registration.

Firstly, you add 17.5 per cent more to your invoices, and as the tax man only collects VAT quarterly, you can earn interest on this money before you hand it over. Secondly, you deduct from that amount any money you have paid out on your purchases. Effectively this means that all the VAT you pay out to suppliers can be reclaimed from the Revenue. As most businesses are VAT-registered and therefore charge VAT, being able to reclaim that VAT can save you hundreds, if not thousands, of pounds. Let me give you an example:

Company 1 (Registered for VAT)

Sales:	4500	Purchases:	2300
VAT on sales:	787.50 (A)	VAT on purchases:	402.50 (B)
Income:	5287.50 (C)	Total paid out:	2702.50

VAT paid to the Revenue is A – B = 385 (D)

Total income is C – D = 4902.50

Company 2 (Not registered for VAT)

Sales:	4500	Purchases:	2300
Total income:	4500	VAT on purchases:	402.50
		Total paid out:	2702.50

Total income is 4500

As you can see, the company that is VAT-registered has a greater income because it has reclaimed the VAT on its purchases. The bigger your business, the more money you are likely to save by registering for VAT.

Being VAT-registered requires a little more discipline with your accounting. Not only do you have to keep your records in good order, but you also need to remember that not all the money in the bank is yours to spend – some of it will be going to the Revenue. The records aren't much more complicated than those you would keep to compile your end-of-year tax return, and just a few hours' work every three months could earn you a lot of money. VAT returns are completed each quarter, and if you complete your return online, you get even longer to pay. For example, if your return covers the three months up until 31 October, you won't have to hand over any money until 12 December. Alternatively, you can agree a flat rate with the Revenue to pay monthly if that helps with your cashflow. All the information you need is available at www.inlandrevenue.gov.uk.

As with every other tax and levy, VAT rates are subject to change.

If your business is affected by VAT, stamp duty, capital gains tax or corporation tax, then you should make sure you watch or listen to the Chancellor deliver his annual Budget. Friends of mine who aren't in business can't believe I actually enjoy hearing the Budget, but when those changes affect the business you're passionate about, the Budget becomes surprisingly fascinating!

|||||||||||||||||||||||||||||||| **CASE STUDY** ||||||||||||||||||||||||||||||

Name: Grant Morgan **Age**: 40
Job: CEO, Louis Kennedy
Qualifications: None
www.louiskennedy.com

I left school at 16 with no real qualifications and went to Barnet College in North London to start a course in law. I only managed two weeks – studying simply wasn't for me, so I found myself a job. Unfortunately, it was packing ties in an unheated warehouse in Hackney during winter! After another lousy job, I thought I'd moved up in the world when I got a job working for my uncle Benny at a trading company in Soho. The company supplied merchandise for promotions, not unlike the free glasses you used to get if you bought enough petrol. Having bought myself what I thought was a nice suit from Topman – it was actually disgusting – on my first day I was sent into a dimly lit basement to assemble torch components for an order. I spent six months assembling those torches, but by the end of six years with the company, I had actually learnt quite a lot about sourcing, manufacturing and trading commercial products. I still wasn't thinking about making a career out of it, though: in my spare time I was involved in hospital radio while writing for a number of satirical publications with my writing partner, Ricky Simmonds. Even though these activities delivered little, if any, income, I secretly hoped I might be able to make a career from them one day.

At 22, I joined a small business gift company supplying branded goods to the corporate sector. It was here that I learnt how not to manage people: I worked for a guy who had a perception of himself that I didn't share, often belittling and deriding his staff (of just two) in public. I knew that if I ever had staff, I would treat them with respect. I could only take his nonsense for so long, and at 23 found myself out of a job.

Although I had managed to buy a flat, I couldn't afford to live in it, so rented it out and lived at home with my parents. I might not have had any money, but neither did I have any responsibilities, so I decided to set up on my own. I was quite excited by the trading process, but generic products didn't do it for me. Creative by nature, I wanted to combine the trading with something more exciting and decided to target the children's sector, as kids' products were fun and had personality. I named my new company Louis Kennedy, which was the pseudonym Ricky and I had been writing under (it's a hybrid of our middle names). My dad was none too pleased: he was convinced that if the business succeeded, Ricky would want his share. However, Ricky remains my best friend – we still write together – and he hasn't mentioned it yet!

Initially, I worked from my bedroom and my then girlfriend Emma (now my wife) gave me my first order. She worked as a retail buyer, and her company needed 100,000 badges for a charitable initiative. She arranged for me to be paid in advance and I then pleaded with my suppliers for 30 days' credit, which they gave me because they knew and trusted me from my previous job. The order was worth £6000, a few thousand of which was my profit.

Then, as now, I ploughed all of that money back into the business. I knew that the likes of Unilever and Kellogg's weren't going to deal with someone working from their bedroom, so I rented what could only be described as a broom cupboard in a building of serviced offices. To establish credibility, I spent that first year picking up contracts from old and new clients alike, and trading the usual range of branded pens, mugs and T-shirts.

While sourcing a product for a client, I came across a clever puzzle that I thought would be perfect for Cadbury's, so I sent it cold to their promotions buyer. Amazingly, she made contact. 'Grant, I really don't like this toy,' she told me over the phone, 'but I do like the idea that you're thinking creatively for us.' So she gave me a brief for their 'Animals' brand. I couldn't believe that the buyer for Cadbury's had called *me* in *my broom cupboard*! I was ecstatic.

I designed a selection of 3D animal-shaped finger crayons and was advised that if she liked the prototype, then she would place an order for at least 500,000 units. The only catch was that I had to fund the prototype personally at a cost of £1,500. I obtained a loan, got the prototype made, and when I showed it to her, she liked it so much that she ordered over 3 million of them! That single contract transformed my business and enabled me to attract other high-profile clients.

Unusually, I quite enjoyed the paperwork. My dad taught me old-fashioned triple-entry bookkeeping, but it was still a steep learning curve. I never had a problem going from the sales during the day to the paperwork and invoices at night – it really helped me to understand my business. Maths had never clicked at school; however, as soon as the figures represented actual money, I discovered that I was surprisingly quite gifted at it.

Over the next few years, I took on staff and the business grew steadily. In 1993, I started an associated business, and in 1997, we eventually outgrew the serviced accommodation. I then bought and converted an old school house, which is still the HQ for all my businesses today.

In 2001, I was running four companies with 30 staff and a healthy turnover when my bank manager visited. 'Do you know that you could lose money this year?' I was pretty stunned, but I instantly knew why. My father, who I was supremely close to, had been diagnosed with pancreatic cancer, and he had been my primary concern. I had taken my eye off the ball and two of my businesses – an online company and a clothing operation – were losing money, only being kept afloat by the other two.

However, I knew exactly what I had to do: I had to close down the two loss-making operations, reduce my operating costs, focus on the core businesses, increase my margins and borrow against the Old School House to inject some much-needed capital into the business. 'I can turn this around,' I told him, 'but I'll need the bank's support.' Unbelievably, he called me the next day to say that they wouldn't be offering me the short-term support I needed. He actually said to me, 'It's probably time you called it a day'!

My brother-in-law, who was an independent financial adviser, introduced me to Barclays, who looked at the businesses, listened to what I had to say and believed in me. 'Nothing would give us more pleasure than to take your business away from NatWest,' they said, and within a year I had turned the loss into a substantial profit and we survived. To this day I have remained loyal to Barclays.

The experience made me reassess where we were going, and although successful, I decided that we needed a differential. I had been working with a number of charities since the late 1990s, both pro bono and commercially, and I told my staff that I thought there was an opportunity to add real value to the charitable sector using our contacts in licensing, brand and retail – not to mention our skills in design and product development. So, in 2002, we started to transform the business and walked away from our previous contracts. Five years on, we are the UK's leading and fastest growing cause-related marketing agency, bringing the charitable and commercial sectors together to raise funds for good causes. It could have been an awful decision, but it worked, and we now work with most of the UK's top 100 charities, including BBC Children In Need and Comic Relief, sourcing and manufacturing products for their campaigns. We receive our fees either from new income derived from our initiatives or from the corporate sector – the money rarely comes from the charities' existing funds. In the past five years we have raised £50 million for good causes in the UK.

I now sit on business-advisory panels for a number of charities and am the majority shareholder in several other businesses – including a children's sticker manufacturer called Purple Peach, with distribution in over 30 countries, a US version called Blue Kangaroo and the watch brand Kurt Zeiss, which is e-tailed globally. Over the next few years, I shall be looking to take my 'corporate and social responsibility' model to the USA, invest in a number of associated businesses and finish a script with Ricky that we've been working on for BBC2.

What's the best advice you've ever had? Be a better listener than you are a talker. I have come to realise that the people who aren't always waiting to chip in and have their say are usually the ones who contribute the most value.

What do you wish you'd known from the start? I believe that most lessons in life come with a little bit of pain, and if I hadn't experienced the pain of making my mistakes, perhaps I wouldn't have such a privileged life today. So I wouldn't change a thing.

What's the one thing you'd say to someone starting their first business? I'd actually say three things. One: know your products or services. And I mean really understand them. Two: know your market and your customers. Three: know your numbers. Business isn't easy, but the mechanics are pretty simple – irrespective of product, service or sector. The basic equation of selling something for more than it costs you, and ensuring that you're left with a margin after you have deducted all your costs, is as straightforward as it gets.

7 Growing your business

Being a successful entrepreneur isn't just about starting a business; it's about growing a business. I always want to get a new business to the stage where it's as valuable without me involved as it is with me at the helm. I'm personally not interested in starting businesses that I will always be tied to: I like to create wealth and then realise my investment.

Over the years, I have seen a lot of entrepreneurs who have started a business only to find themselves on a hamster wheel. Often they get up early, work a lot more than their socks off and go to bed shattered every night after a 14-hour day. No matter how passionate you are about your business, after a few years of working like that, you'll start to resent it. So this chapter is all about getting your business into the kind of shape that means you can either employ people to run it for you or sell it for a lot more money than you put into it.

There are three ways to grow a business: reduce your costs, find more customers, or get your existing customers to pay you more money. Of course, implementing those kinds of changes isn't always easy, but by constantly monitoring your progress and by staying alert to opportunities, you can make growth a natural part of your business.

Reviewing the situation

Every entrepreneur needs to set aside some time to take stock, and as it is so easy to just charge ahead, I think it is worth formalising your review process. In the early days, every month isn't too often, and as you move forward, every three months is probably about right. So get your diary out, and set aside an afternoon or an evening when you will sit down and take a good hard look at your business. Close monitoring of your growth usually leads to bigger profits.

You should ask everyone who's close to the business to join you – your mentor, key members of staff and perhaps your professional advisers – and let them know that you want to hear everything they've got to say, even if it's negative. At these regular meetings, you should go over and revise your original SWOT analysis (see Chapter 2, page 60). Together, I think there are five key questions you should ask yourselves:

1 What are we getting right?

2 What's not performing well enough?

3 What have we overlooked?

4 What have we learnt?

5 Where's the opportunity?

1 What are we getting right?

If there is something that you know you are doing well – perhaps because of good customer feedback, or because of better than expected sales figures – then work out why and you can start doing more of the same in other areas of your work. If you discover that one part of your business is particularly well managed, then you can either give that manager more responsibilities or ask other managers to replicate their techniques. You shouldn't just give yourself a pat on the back: this meeting is about making progress, and it is important that successes are analysed in a way that lets you build on them.

2 What's not performing well enough?

When you did your original fag-packet analysis, and later when you wrote your business plan, you mapped out the shape and size of your business. Now is the time to take those documents out of the filing cabinet and examine them to see where reality is falling short of your predictions. It's time to be brutal – it might be your management skills that aren't cutting it, or your salesperson might not be up to the job. If you manage your stock well enough, it should be easy to see what's not selling. Is there a reason for that, and does that mean there are some products and services you should stop offering?

Whatever it is you discover, you have to make a decision between putting it right or ditching it. In the early days of a business, it can be better to focus on a few key products and services, and diversify later on. Streamlining now doesn't mean you can't expand in the future, and if something is problematic and holding you back, you may be better off without it.

3 What have we overlooked?

Your business plan will come in handy for this too. Is there something you set out to do, but that got lost along the way? It can be so easy to concentrate on what's going well, or to be so overwhelmed by sorting out the things that are going wrong, that sometimes even quite fundamental things get left by the wayside. Maybe you always thought you would renegotiate with your suppliers when you were a bit more established, perhaps for a better rate, or maybe for a longer credit period. This is your opportunity to do some housekeeping and make sure that nasty surprises aren't building up in forgotten corners of your business.

4 What have we learnt?

The different members of your team will have learnt different things – perhaps that sales were harder than anticipated, or your target market is younger than you expected, or the admin side of things is less time-consuming than you predicted. After a few months in business, you should know things about your capabilities, your product, your market, your customers and your rivals that you didn't know when you started. Ask yourself if this means you need to adjust your business. I'll give you an example: one of the big lessons I learnt after I'd built a couple of health clubs was that building staircases and corridors was just as expensive per square foot as building usable space like fitness rooms and changing rooms. So I asked my architect to design future clubs with as little dead space as possible, which saved tens of thousands of pounds each time we built a new club.

By now you should also have a good idea how you are getting customers. Is it through recommendation, media coverage, marketing or Google? Are you spending money on marketing that doesn't work?

It amazes me how often people tell me that they were doing all right until a rival launched, the market cooled or any number of excuses that basically come down to one thing: they didn't move with the times. New businesses live and die on their ability to respond to change, and the more you harness what you've learnt, the greater your chances of success will be.

5 Where's the opportunity?

Before you started your company, I recommended that you read every bit of literature that was relevant to your business. Whether that's a trade publication, the business pages of your newspaper or online newsletters, staying plugged into your industry is absolutely crucial to make sure your company grows in the right direction. You should always be on the look-out for trends and changes in technology, the economy or legislation that might have an impact on your business.

If you are getting a lot of repeat business, does this mean you could charge more for your products? Are there additional services you can offer your existing customers that would increase your turnover without a hike in marketing costs?

The clues to making your business a success are all around you. Some of them are buried in your sales figures, some of them you'll find when you start networking at industry events, others are plastered all over the newspapers. Wherever they are, it is your job to identify them and use them to grow your business.

When Bannatyne Health Clubs acquired 24 clubs from Hilton Hotels in 2006, we asked exactly these sorts of questions and discovered all kinds of inefficiencies in their operation. By making a few simple changes – not offering free towels and doing away with day passes for friends – we have massively improved the profitability of those clubs. If Hilton had applied the same rigour, they might have decided those clubs were too valuable to sell.

Getting the most out of your customers

One of the simplest ways of growing your business is to get repeat business from the same clients. Part of your review should concentrate on finding ways to sell more of your company's products or services to the same customers. There is a very good reason for this: acquiring new customers can take time and may only happen after a costly advertising campaign. You already know how to reach your existing customers, so all you have to work out is how to give them more of what they want.

The best way to find out what they want is to ask them. If you run a shop, ask them what else you could stock. If you run premises, a suggestions box might yield results, and if you have their email addresses, send them a questionnaire. Offering a prize draw for completed entries will boost the number of responses (and this doesn't have to be a trip to Jamaica, it can simply be money off their next order – something that doesn't cost you very much). I have a poster with my email address on it in each of my clubs: if my members can suggest something that I can improve or put right, then I want to know about it. One change that came about from a member's suggestion was the introduction of family changing rooms. A member told me she felt uncomfortable undressing in front of the ten-year-old son of another member – particularly because she was his teacher!

You can start by using your common sense. If someone buys their envelopes from you, perhaps they'll need some pens too. If your café has a good breakfast trade, how can you get them back in at lunchtime? It's the equivalent of the counter staff at McDonald's asking if 'you want fries with that'. As you move your business forward, you need to add some items to your menu that complement your main offering.

You may feel that business is so good that you could put your prices up and increase your turnover at a stroke. This may be obvious, but it can cause problems: what if people are only buying from you because you're the cheapest? You could suddenly lose your customers, and there's always a chance you won't get them back. If it really is necessary to put up your prices – perhaps rents have gone up, or costs, or a crucial exchange rate has affected your trade – explaining this to your customers will help them to take it on the chin.

It's also possible to put up your prices for some customers and not others. Depending on your line of work, you might be able to tier your offering into bronze, silver and gold levels that allow you to charge some clients more for different types of service, or different sorts of products. The obvious example of this is in my health clubs where we have peak and off-peak memberships and different rates for the over-55s who use the clubs during the day. Generally, people are willing to pay more for one of three things: personal service, quality of the products and convenience. Sometimes, making those improvements costs you very little, but they still allow you to put your prices up while simultaneously deepening your relationship with your customer.

Marketing

Reaching out to more potential customers and clients is the single most effective way of building your business, but finding them and getting your message to them can be very expensive. This section is all about getting the biggest bang from your marketing buck and making sure that you use the full range of marketing tools available to you.

It's surprisingly easy to waste money on marketing if you don't know what you're doing. As soon as you start employing PR agencies or buying advertising space, the bills quickly start to mount, but the internet – and particularly email – has made doing some effective marketing yourself a lot easier.

Introduce a friend

There's a very strong likelihood that your customers and clients know other people who would like to use your product or service. It makes sense: if your customers are new parents, the chances are that they know other new parents who will like your baby products. If you can encourage each of them to introduce a friend to your business, then you can double your sales at a stroke. Not only is using your existing customer base a cost-effective way of recruiting new clients because you know how and where to reach them, but because they know you they can *endorse* you. They become the best kind of sales force: they become *advocates*. We are all much more likely to try something new if a friend has recommended it.

However you communicate with your clients, whether online, face to face or over the phone, you need to devise ways of encouraging them to recruit new customers on your behalf. Can you give them money off their next order, enhanced services, one month free? Choose something that will work for your type of business and your customers.

To make these referrals really work, you also need to give the new cus tomers a reason to buy from you too. Can you give them a time-limited offer, a discount or a freebie of some sort? You may be thinking this is financial insanity, giving a discount to two customers, but if your profit margins are wide enough, you can absorb the discount quite painlessly (and if you've done your sensitivity analysis, you should know exactly how much you can reduce your prices by and still make a profit). And, of course, that discount is only for one order: all their subsequent orders will be at full price.

You then need to devise a way to get the referrals. You could give your customers vouchers to give to their friends (with a code on it that allows you to award the incentive to the right customer), or give them a code on their next invoice to circulate that could be used by any of their friends. There are any number of solutions, and the really great thing is that it doesn't cost you very much to do, possibly just the price of getting some vouchers printed. You only take the hit on your income when you make a sale, meaning this doesn't leave a big red hole in your cashflow.

Affiliate schemes

Affiliate schemes operate on a pretty simple concept: if you bring me customers, I'll give you a slice of the money they spend with me. Such schemes have become very standard online, and there's really no reason why they can't work for offline businesses too – they just require a bit of management.

If you operate online, affiliate schemes work by giving other websites an advert for your website, and if their users click on it and then buy something from you, you automatically credit your affiliate's account with their percentage. These percentages are typically around 5 or 10 per cent, and they can be far more lucrative for your affiliates than standard banner advertising. Your affiliate will tend to give you a big push, because the more people they send to your site, the more income they stand to make.

It's great for you too. You only have to offer a tiny discount and only ever take the hit when you make a sale, so not a single penny of your marketing budget is spent on reaching people who will never become your customers. If you were to sell fishing gear, for example, you might offer an affiliate deal to all those fishing forums and fan sites that could send their users to your site rather than your rivals' sites. In the real world, affiliate schemes can be implemented using vouchers, promotional codes or through negotiated contracts.

Whoever built your website should be capable of setting up an affiliate scheme, but if they can't help, I am reliably informed that it's a fairly standard script for an experienced programmer to write. There are also plenty of websites with advice on starting an affiliate scheme.

Of course, you should also think about becoming an affiliate yourself and earning income from referring your customers to other businesses.

Leaflets and posters

If your business is a local one, perhaps the most effective form of marketing is a leaflet drop. You can get flyers printed for a few hundred pounds and get friends and family to deliver them for nothing. Alternatively, Royal Mail can deliver for a pretty cost-effective fee, or a specialist flyers agency can do the job. Be prepared to send leaflets out more than once, perhaps every couple of months, to get the best results.

And while you're at the printers, get a handful of posters and ask local retailers and residents if you can put one in their window. They might ask for a couple of quid, but it's an incredibly cheap and effective form of advertising.

Viral email

I'm sure we've all been forwarded emails by friends who think we might be interested in a particular website, survey or YouTube clip. Viral marketing campaigns set out to create content that people will spontaneously forward on to everyone in their mailbox.

To use a bit of marketing jargon, you need to create something *contagious*. Can you make a funny video that somehow promotes your business, or write a joke, or set a puzzle that can only be solved if people get in touch with you? Every couple of months there's a story about a business

217

that has been catapulted to prominence because of a video on YouTube or a networking campaign on sites such as Facebook. If you can't come up with something creative, you can always fall back on traditional marketing ploys – like the first 100 customers who bring a copy of this email get something for free, or all respondents get put into a draw for a fabulous holiday, or get money off.

Be careful when offering money-off vouchers, however, as sometimes viral campaigns can be very successful and if you are issuing the discount at a loss, you could end up in trouble. Losing a few pounds on the odd sale won't hurt you, but if you have to honour thousands of customers who rightly claim their discount, you could be seriously out of pocket!

Piggybacking

Many different businesses want to reach the same customers, and if you can find a company that already reaches the customers you want to convert, then perhaps you can find a way to 'piggyback' the other firm's marketing reach.

Obviously, you're unlikely to come to an arrangement with a rival, but there will be allied businesses with whom you can set up a reciprocal deal. For instance, If you're setting up a renovations business, a large proportion of your clients will have recently moved house. So think laterally about who deals with these people – estate agents, conveyancers, removals companies – and see if there's a way you can work together.

It can be as simple as inserting a flyer into another company's brochure, or making your literature available at someone else's event, or on someone else's reception desk.

Not only does this let you build up a relationship with other companies who need to reach your market, you can be fairly sure that a high proportion of people who see your marketing are likely to be potential customers. You therefore waste very little money.

PR

Public relations agencies use the media to reach as many of your potential customers as possible. They place stories about your company in the papers, on radio and occasionally on TV too. The key word is 'stories' – the media aren't often interested in factual information; they want a tale they can entertain their audiences with. Over the years, I've posed for many publicity photos doing stupid things, but they have always got my story in the paper.

PR agencies usually charge you a monthly fee for doing things like writing press releases, arranging photo shoots, setting up 'stunts' to create a story, approaching the media and handling any press enquiries. Their fee can be anything between £1000 pcm for a small outfit to £10,000 a month for a high-profile operator like Max Clifford. Most people who are just a little bit media savvy are capable of doing some, or all, of the jobs of a PR agency, but what they might not have are the PR agency's contacts. A good agent should know which journalists will be interested in which sorts of stories and be able to place them in the right publications with a handful of carefully considered phone calls. An amateur can waste a lot of time writing press releases that don't contain the right information and sending them to the wrong sorts of journalists.

Whether you handle your PR yourself or outsource it to a specialist, you need to come up with a few stories for the media. Only the smallest local paper will see 'New business opens' as a story. Everyone else will want something a bit meatier, and 'New shop opened by local celebrity' will get you more coverage. The sorts of things that get journalists interested are: money, so always include a figure ('Hotel opens after £1 million re-fit' will get their attention ahead of 'Hotel re-opens'), a charitable angle (especially if you've done some fundraising in fancy dress as that makes a good photo), surveys ('Results show our sausages were the tastiest'), tales of triumph over tragedy and quirkiness ('I employ two of my school teachers').

You need to tailor your PR to the publication you want coverage in, as the sorts of stories a trade magazine would carry will be different from those that appeal to a national radio station. Look at the sorts of stories the different papers and stations carry, and see how you can create exactly the right noises that will make them pay attention.

To make your PR more effective, follow this advice:

* Make sure you speak to the right person. There's no point sending a press release to the BBC: identify which show or shows you think are likely to talk to you, then call reception and ask to speak to the relevant production team. The same goes for newspapers: sending something to *The Times* isn't nearly as effective as sending something to a specific journalist. If there's a journalist on a particular paper who regularly writes about your field, you'll probably be able to work out their email address just by knowing their name.

* Give media companies enough time. If you're launching a new product tomorrow, there's very little point contacting journalists today. Magazines and radio shows have lead-in times, and they often decide on content weeks, if not months, in advance. Phone up and ask when is the best time to send them information.

* Make sure your press releases contain real news. If you can think of a stunt that will make people take notice, then you can make a story to tempt them with. Journalists like stories, and more than that, they like exclusive stories that their rivals don't have.

* Make sure your press releases are well written and include all the information a journalist needs to write a short story without contacting you. You should always include a quote from the founder of the company as this makes it look as if they've interviewed you.

* Never underestimate the power of the photo, and bear in mind that sometimes journalists can't run a story unless they can illustrate it too. So put on a silly hat, say cheese and get yourself some coverage.

* Build up a relationship with useful journalists, and make yourself available to be quoted for any story they're working on. My name used to be in the paper all the time as journalists would call me up for a quote on anything from how a proposed development would affect local business to what I thought of a local beauty contest.

Advertising

I've left this until last because it's the most expensive and it's pretty rare for a new company to have the kind of money needed for a sustained radio, TV or print campaign.

If you're operating a local service, then you will obviously want to advertise locally, not nationally. If your customers all work in the hotel industry, then you will want to advertise in a trade publication rather than a national newspaper. If you want to reach kids, then you should be advertising online, not in a Sunday supplement.

Once you've worked out where you should be advertising, you need to think about what you will be advertising. Is it just the fact you exist, or the fact you've got a sale on or have some new merchandise in stock? Advertising, like businesses themselves, works best when it solves people's problems, and you'll do well if you can present your company as the solution. Whether you do this with humour or just by stating the facts will depend on your business and your market.

Call up the radio station, or publication, or website you want to advertise on and ask how much they charge. You can probably estimate that the real figure they expect you to pay is somewhere between two-thirds and half of what they first tell you, and the more ads you place with them, the cheaper each ad will become. Conventional wisdom says that a customer needs to see or hear an ad at least seven times before they will remember you. As people don't listen to the radio all day, and they don't buy every edition of a paper, you are going to have to budget for a lot of ads.

Do your sums very carefully before you commit to an advertising campaign, and if you think you can afford it, it's probably worth talking to a specialist advertising agency. Even if you don't end up using them, you will get a lot of advice and ideas just from your preliminary meetings with them. They can advise you on the creative content of your adverts, as well as the strategy for getting them seen by as many potential customers as possible.

At Bannatyne Health Clubs, we use advertising very sparingly. When we open a new club, we pay for a prominent ad or two in the local paper in our opening week, and after that only if we have special offers and are on a recruitment drive. Even though we're a national chain, I don't see any point in a national advertising campaign, as people in Surrey aren't going to join my club in Durham. The secret to effective advertising is to target your marketing spend as tightly as possible, otherwise you could waste thousands of pounds reaching people who have no need of your products or services.

Building a team

Few businesses get to grow to a decent size unless they employ a good team of people, and your ability to assemble an A team could make the difference between fortune and failure. Taking on staff is a big step, and a lot of entrepreneurs suffer from a kind of culture shock when the company that has previously just been them and their friends suddenly welcomes a stranger through the door.

Staff requirements will change as your company grows. At first, new businesses thrive when a small team gets caught up in the challenge and people don't realise they're working 15-hour days because it's so much fun. In the early days, you need people who will muck in and do everything from answer the phone to help raise finance. As your business grows, you will need people who specialise in particular areas, and as those areas expand, you will need to find people with management skills to make sure everyone's efforts are coordinated.

New members of staff have a very different perspective from the founders. They're unlikely to have a financial stake in the company's success beyond their salary, and they're less likely to work long hours unless they get something other than money out of it. The first employees in a new company are motivated by different things, perhaps the opportunity to get experience in an area their previous employer wouldn't have given them a chance at, or the opportunity for early promotion. Understanding what motivates your employees is the secret to getting the most out of them.

Hiring staff can be time-consuming and expensive; I've found it can often be cheaper and quicker to train existing staff for new roles than it is to bring in someone from outside. If you have a talented team, you should always look to promote from within rather than recruit from elsewhere.

Talent is the most difficult resource to manage, and the most successful people in business are those who have found ways of letting their staff shine in roles they were born to do. Perhaps, instead of looking for a new recruit who can handle your sales, you should let an able team member move into sales, and recruit someone cheaper to take on some of their admin tasks. Staff are any business's most expensive resource, and your job is to manage that resource as cost-effectively as possible.

Assessing your needs

New business owners often recruit their first members of staff out of panic because they are just so damn busy. They know they need someone – anyone – who can share the workload, and this means they rarely get the best person for the job.

To avoid this, you need to work out why you're so busy and which bits of your current workload can best be taken on by someone else. This shouldn't be the parts of your job that you enjoy least; it should be the functions where you are least able. You then need to work out how those functions can be packaged together to make a proper job for an outsider.

You shouldn't just recruit reactively however. Pro-active recruitment where you create and fill a role that will transform your business is also important. If you can't grow your business on your own, identify the jobs that need to be done that would move things forward and start to build up a profile of the person that would fill that position.

Remember the test in Chapter 3 that indicated where your natural aptitudes lie? That test (see page 88) was based on the kinds of profiling employers often do to find out where candidates will fit into their existing team, and the secret to building a strong team is to make sure you have people who fit into as many of those categories as possible.

You probably scored highly in one or two categories, so in an ideal world, you would want other members of your team to have complementary aptitudes from the other categories. Every company needs its creative geniuses and dynamic leaders, but it also needs people who bother to read the small print, and who will stay with a task until it's done. When you only have a handful of people in your company, getting the personality balance right can be as important as getting the skills balance right. A team of four that works well together can achieve just as much as a team of eight that pulls in opposite directions and is undermined by personality conflicts. When you appoint a new member of staff, you don't want to rely solely on instinct – a candidate should have the skills and attributes you originally set out to recruit – but it's important the new team member will fit into your company's culture.

This doesn't mean you should only employ your friends, or 'yes men'; it just means that sometimes the best-qualified candidate isn't actually the best person for your company. It may be that you need a terrier who will bark at you when deadlines are missed rather than someone you'd get along with. The key thing is to weigh up a candidate's skills with their personality and attitudes.

Who do you know?

When you're job-hunting, everyone says, 'It's not what you know, it's who you know,' and it's true when you're recruiting too. The best candidate might be very close at hand, possibly someone who's already working for you, or maybe someone you've come across while you've been launching your business. Was there someone who impressed you at the bank you dealt with, or at one of your suppliers, or a client? If you've come across an able operator – especially one who already works in your industry – then poaching them for your own company can give you a real boost.

You might not personally know the ideal candidate, but you might well know someone who does, and nothing beats an endorsement from someone you trust. Often, your best contacts for recruiting by word of mouth are your clients, as they might well be in regular contact with similar companies to yours. Ask a trusted client if there's anyone you should poach.

Your mentor should be a good source of information about recruitment too, and if you've chosen them for their sector experience, this is when they become worth their weight in gold. Not only will you find candidates that have been personally recommended, but recruiting this way is often quicker and certainly cheaper than advertising or using an agency.

Recruiting

If you can't find an appropriate candidate through personal contacts, then you need to formalise your search, and you essentially have two options: to advertise or use a recruitment agency.

Advertising

Recruitment advertising can be expensive, especially if you are looking for skilled candidates through the specialist and national press. It's much cheaper to place an ad in a local paper, but this is more suitable for casual or unskilled labour.

Wherever you place your ad, and whatever the position, it's important that you give prospective candidates all the information they need to a) decide if it's the right position for them, and b) make an application. Don't just say 'chef wanted' and expect lots of applications. You need to specify the day-to-day responsibilities, the qualifications and experience you are expecting, and the kind of environment they will be working in. You also need to give an indication of the salary you will be offering.

If you've never placed a recruitment ad before, it's easy to throw money away. I would suggest that you think about the sort of publication you will advertise in, and then study the ads other employers are placing in that publication. Put yourself in the jobseeker's shoes and ask yourself which companies sound attractive, and which positions seem appealing.

Then make sure that potential candidates know how to apply. Do they need to send a CV, a covering letter, references and/or examples of previous work? Do you want to receive things in the post or by email? Make sure your instructions are clear.

Agencies

Finding staff through a recruitment agency is the most expensive way of recruiting, but that's not the only reason why you should use it as a last resort. In my experience, the kind of people agencies have on their books tend to be opportunistic jobseekers, the kind of people who lodge their CV with an agency in the hope that something better will turn up.

Agencies tend to be good at recruiting for skilled positions where the key factor in a candidate's suitability is their professional qualification. But when you're looking for an all-rounder to help you in the early days, essentially an odd-shaped employee for an odd-shaped hole, their rigid systems and forms can miss the best candidates.

However, there are bad agencies and good agencies, and you may find yourself working with one that completely understands your needs and almost plays the role of an external Human Resources department. A good agency will listen while you explain what you're after and will help you identify the sorts of candidates you can hope to attract. They will then see who is on their books, and if there are no suitable candidates, they will advertise or head-hunt.

Agencies come into their own when you just don't have the time to handle your recruitment needs. They can save you hours by sifting through CVs and having preliminary chats with candidates to assess their suitability. A good recruitment consultant who views your company with the right perspective might also make you realise that you need to hire someone with completely different skills to those you thought you needed. If they're experienced, they should also have advice on where to poach staff from, or what your rivals offer in terms of salaries and benefits.

Agencies charge for their advertising, but they really make their money by charging you a commission that is typically 25 to 30 per cent of the candidate's first year's salary. Terms differ from agency to agency, but if you're on a tight budget, their fees can really hurt. Especially if the candidate resigns after a couple of months and you need to start the process again.

Determining salaries

Deciding how much to pay employees is a delicate business. As a general rule, you should keep your salaries as low as possible. Nothing eats into your cashflow and your capital like salaries, and if you can shave a few grand off your salary bill each month, it might just keep you afloat for a couple of extra months, and that could be all the time you need to land the contract that transforms your business.

As an employer, you have a whole range of other incentives you can use to motivate your team instead of money. Survey after survey shows that people don't move jobs to get a better salary; they do it because they don't feel valued. Offering people a position where they will make a difference, where they will have fun and where their hard work won't go unappreciated has been proved to be as good an incentive as a pay rise for most workers.

However, if you don't pay the going rate, you will have a high staff turnover and will be constantly diverted from running your business with recruitment headaches. So how do you find out what's a fair salary? If you already work in the industry, the chances are that you probably have a good idea, and if you know other employers in the industry – perhaps former colleagues – you could ask them what they pay. They might just tell you.

If you've been in contact with a recruitment agency, they should be able to give you a ballpark figure, but this will probably be slightly higher than the industry standard (after all, they are on a commission). You can make your own assessment by scouring the recruitment ads and seeing what salaries are being offered for similar positions. In addition, some trade unions have a list of pay settlements and can advise on the going rate in some professions.

● ● ● ● ● **BANNATYNE'S BOOTCAMP** ● ● ● ● ●

Incentives

I believe people should be rewarded for doing their job well and I use bonuses as an incentive to get the best out of the people I employ. When I ran my care homes, every member of the team got an annual bonus when the homes achieved a 98 per cent occupancy rate. Everyone on the team shared the bonus, from the nurses to the cleaning staff, so that everyone felt they were part of a team. I have a similar scheme at my health clubs now.

When I use lawyers, I will often strike a deal with them that means they will only get part of their fixed fee if the negotiations are concluded to my advantage and on time. When I employ builders, I incentivise them to save money by sharing any savings with them if they can use faster construction methods or source a cheaper supplier. Not only does this save me money on the initial building project, but I can use that knowledge to save money on all future building projects.

Wherever possible, I want to pay for results and not effort, so whoever you are dealing with, try to find a way to incentivise them to do their work at the standard you expect.

● ●

The interview process

In an ideal world, a manager in business would get the same opportunity as a football manager to observe new team members in action before offering them a contract. Sadly, we have the interview process instead, which basically means you spend between 30 minutes and an hour with someone before committing to working with them for (possibly) years to come. It's therefore important that you get the most you can out of the process.

A good interview starts with good preparation, and that starts with making sure you've asked applicants for the right sort of information. For most positions, this tends to be no more than a CV and a covering letter, although in some creative professions it's also standard to include copies of previous work. As CVs have a reputation for telling little white lies, you need to read them with a magnifying glass to find clues about an applicant's suitability.

You should draw up a wish list of experience, qualifications and attitudes that your ideal candidate would have. You should then judge each application against this wish list and invite the best candidates in for an interview. However, sometimes the best candidates don't have the best

CVs, and this is when the covering letter can be very valuable. A candidate who recognises that they don't have the x and y you asked for in your advert, but has z instead might bring something different to your team. Anyone who's taken the time in their letter to show that they know something about your company, or who expresses a desire to work for a new company, would leap up my score sheet.

Once you've drawn up the list of people you want to invite for interview, take a couple of hours to do your research on them. Put their names into Google, search for them on Facebook or MySpace: it's amazing how many people put their details on these networking sites and the information they offer about themselves can help you assess them. You might find out something that convinces you they are the perfect candidate, or a waste of your time.

If it's possible, ask someone else to conduct the interviews with you, especially if you have never interviewed people before. Your mentor would be an ideal choice, but any friend who has experience in recruitment could be valuable: not only does it take some of the pressure off you, but you then have someone to discuss candidates with after the interview.

Ahead of the interview, draw up a list of questions you want to ask the candidates, and during the interview make copious notes, as afterwards there's a danger they'll all merge into one. Avoid asking general questions like 'Tell me about your career', and instead ask questions that reveal how they behave in given situations. For instance: 'Give me an example of a time when you've taken the lead', or 'Give me an example of a time when you have overcome challenges in your career.' If you are carrying out several interviews in a day, be sure to leave time between interviews to complete your note-making.

In a new company, having a team that's prepared to drop everything and work late until an order is met can be the difference between success and failure. Ask about their willingness to muck in: what you don't want is a clock-watcher who will do little more than drain your cashflow. I think it's also useful to ask a candidate where they would like their career to take them: are they ambitious, will they move on in six months, what is their ideal role in your organisation? Remember, you're not just trying to fill a hole in your workforce; you want people who can grow with your company and perhaps take on a different role in the future.

You don't have to decide after one interview. It's perfectly all right to ask a candidate back a second time, perhaps with someone else on hand to ask some different questions. It may be that after two interviews, you're still not sure, and this might present you with a real dilemma. Employing the wrong person in a small team can be dangerous: their flaws and shortcomings could pull a small operation off course, and you may come to the conclusion that – for the time being – you are better off without a new member of staff. Employment law these days gives employees an armful of rights, and getting rid of someone who doesn't fit in is both difficult and costly once they've completed a trial period.

Offering someone a job

When you've chosen a candidate, you need to know exactly what you are expecting them to do in return for their salary and, perhaps more importantly, they do too. You should write a formal job description setting out the responsibilities, targets and skills involved in the position. The candidate should be told who they will report to and how their effectiveness will be measured. I think it's also worthwhile to give some indication of the opportunities for advancement the job will provide.

After an interview, you can bet that the candidates will jump every time their phone rings, and I think you have a duty to inform the successful and unsuccessful as soon as possible. It is standard practice to phone the successful candidate and write to those who have missed out (although you should wait to post those letters until your chosen candidate has accepted the position). When you call your first choice, offer them the position and state the salary. Then tell them you will email them a detailed job description and ask them to accept the position within a decent timeframe, say 24 hours. If they turn you down, you need to look at the runners-up.

Expect the best candidates to negotiate over the salary. Especially if they are filling senior management or sales roles. To be honest, you probably want them to negotiate with you, otherwise you might be about to hire a doormat, but that doesn't mean you have to blow your budget. They need to understand that you are a small company and while there isn't the money in the bank now, there should be an opportunity for an early review if they meet their targets and help the company grow. Or perhaps you could offer a bonus once they've proved themselves. If salary is a sticking point, and you really want to secure this person's service, then perhaps concede a little, but see if you can offer them other things instead. Perhaps the ability to work from home one day a week, or a better job title, or extra responsibilities would swing it?

Once they have accepted the job, you should give them the terms and conditions of their position – things like trial periods, notice periods, disciplinary procedure, formal reviews.

Working with your team

I believe that delegation is essential to good teamwork and this might therefore be the most important section of this book. I certainly believe that my ability to delegate has been one of the most important factors in my success, and if you can learn to delegate too, then it will free you up to run your company more dynamically.

Effective delegation involves setting targets, empowering staff to meet their targets, and setting a deadline for a review of those targets (see page 84). That's the easy bit. The difficult bit is trusting them to do their work. If I had a pound for every time I've had a flustered entrepreneur complain to me that in the time it takes them to explain the job to someone they could have done it better themselves, then I'd be a lot richer than I am.

It's true, training and supporting new staff can be time-consuming, but if you don't do it, you can never move forward. However, I have observed that what can be a far bigger waste of time is constant interference by the boss. All those 'How are you getting on?' chats, or those 'You might find it easier if…' pep talks are not only distracting, they can undermine the new employee. Giving part of the responsibility for your company to an outsider requires you to make adjustments, and no longer being in complete control is something a lot of people tell me they find difficult. So here are my tips on how to get the most out of your team:

* Make it clear what each person is responsible for.

* Make it clear how important their job is to the rest of company.

* Give each team member realistic targets (selling so many products, coming up with a marketing campaign, finding a more reliable supplier).

* Give them a deadline for achieving their target.

* Give them the means they need to do this (the time, the raw materials, etc.).

* Let them know they can come to you if they have difficulties.

* *Then just let them get on with their job without interference.*

As the company grows, effective delegation is aided by a clear management structure. Everyone in the company needs to know who their line manager is. I believe the best structure for a large company is the one that makes most sense – the pyramid structure, with workers at the bottom reporting to a handful of managers, who report to a couple of divisional managers, who, in turn, report to the boss. This way, each manager isn't tied down by too many responsibilities. The boss sets the targets, the divisional managers assess how their team will achieve those targets, and the managers are responsible for making sure the team delivers. As the boss, I don't need to know how they meet their targets, because that's not my job. I just need to know it gets done.

If you are working in the same office as one of your employees, it can be very difficult to hold your tongue when you hear them on the phone saying things you wouldn't say if you were making the same call. But look at it from their point of view. It's hard enough starting a new job without the boss jumping in all the time. You need to let people make mistakes. You need to let people do things differently. After all, it's not just your company any more: if they're properly motivated, your staff should feel like it's theirs too.

> **'** *Effective delegation involves setting targets, empowering staff to meet their targets, and setting a deadline for a review of those targets.* **'**

● ● ● ● ● **BANNATYNE'S BOOTCAMP** ● ● ● ● ●

Keep it in-house

I never understand businesses that outsource their maintenance, or their cleaning, or their bookkeeping. If one of my clubs isn't clean, I want the manager to be able to a) know who is responsible, and b) have the authority to get it cleaned. If we used an outside cleaning agency, the cleaner wouldn't report to the manager, but to their own boss outside our company. And as you don't just pay the cleaner's wages, you also pay the agency that employs them a fee on top, I think outsourcing is often a waste of money.

You can't control the agency's recruitment policy, and you could end up with a different person on your premises every day. The consequence being that no one knows each other, team spirit breaks down, and no one feels responsible for their actions.

● ●

IIIIIIIIIIIIIIIIIIIIIIIIIIIIIIIII **CASE STUDY** IIIIIIIIIIIIIIIIIIIIIIIIIIIIIIII

Name: Damaris Evans **Age**: 31
Job: Founder, Damaris 'sine qua non'
Qualifications: Degree from Central St Martin's College
www.damaris.co.uk

I've always been interested in fashion, and although it was my hobby growing up, I always assumed I'd end up with a traditional profes-sional career in an office. However, my love of fashion took me to Central St Martin's, where I studied women's fashion design with print. When I graduated, I thought I wanted to work in one of the top fashion houses, but I realised while I was at college that it is actually quite dif-ficult to get hands-on experience in those companies, and you can easily find yourself making the tea. You also have to play the corpo-rate game, and I've never been great with authority and realised I wanted to be in control. My course involved a work-experience place-ment at a fashion house called Favourbrook and even in a smaller company it was still difficult to have an idea and then be allowed to follow through on it: I never wanted to compromise on the quality of the final product, but the commercial realities meant I was often asked to do so.

I actually stayed with Favourbrook's for a year and half to co-design collections for New York Fashion Week before going back to college to finish my degree. I knew by then that I wanted to design lingerie, and as there wasn't a company doing what I wanted to do, I was going to have to start out on my own. In the beginning, I was driven – and guided – by one principle: to always do the best. I didn't care about the expense, only the product: if a pair of knickers ended up costing £3000, that was OK. The problem I had was that there wasn't a market for such luxury – before I launched, no one had sold a pair of knickers for more than £100 – so not only did I have to create the product, but I had to create the market too.

I had pretty limited funds, so I applied to the Prince's Trust for a loan. They put me in touch with the Portobello Business Centre near where I live in West London, and they helped me put together a business plan. I went to see them every couple of weeks, and they guided me through the process, which involved preparing financial forecasts and conducting a bit of market research. It took a couple of months to complete the business plan, and the funny thing is, I know so much more now that I feel I could write my next one in an evening! Although it was something I only did to get the loan, I found it helpful to outline certain areas and to structure the finances. The problem the Trust had with my application was that I couldn't prove there was a market, so it really came down to whether they believed in me or not. They offered me a loan of £5000 to be paid back monthly.

To keep costs down, I decided to print the fabric myself and hand-dyed the elastic, but it was virtually impossible to find someone to make the garments for me. I found one guy, but he proved difficult to work with, and eventually I found an Italian factory at a lingerie trade fair that had a fabulous track record. I told them I was launching a new label and they agreed to make some samples for me, so I took my fabrics out to Italy and ended up becoming great friends with the factory owners. They made about 60 pieces for my first collection, and when I came back to London, my priority was getting these fantastic samples into the hands of the buyers.

I can't stress enough just how different Damaris was to other lingerie. The garment that got most of the attention was my bow knicker that has a big bow designed to be visible over the top of a pair of jeans. No one had seen anything like it. I called up Selfridges and made an appointment to see their lingerie buyer, which is something I don't think I'd be able to do if I started now because the market is so crowded, but in 2001 she was excited to hear about something new.

I cycled to Selfridges with the garments in a basket over the handlebars, and although the buyer really loved the products, she couldn't agree to a wholesale price of £40. She thought that should be the retail price. 'But that's what it costs,' I told her. She said it might help if I could get some press coverage.

I'd always known press support would be crucial, so I had already started approaching the fashion magazines. I'd had an amazing response, but the lead-in times of fashion magazines meant I would have to wait a couple of months before I had any press cuttings to show the retailers. Damaris was featured in *Vogue*, we had a double-page spread in the *Evening Standard*, and a lot of the top stylists started using us. The fact that we were so expensive – most of our lines were £120–30, and some hand-finished items cost up to £3000 – helped us get attention. I also had a show at London Fashion Week, and when the buyer from Selfridges saw the coverage, she invited me back and placed an order. The coverage also helped us get stocked in shops like Harvey Nichols and Liberty, and our turnover for our first season was £30,000, which I thought was incredible.

We had our fair share of problems, though, most of which were to do with production. The factory in Italy that had made the samples said they couldn't handle the finish I was after on a commercial scale, so I looked around for other factories. We got let down, and boxes of fabric would be returned to us, with the garments unmade, a week before we were due to deliver to the shops. I was using couture fabrics and techniques used on clothing: it wasn't just a case of zimming a piece of elastic on to some nylon. They all told me it was too complicated, so I had to call in everyone I knew who could sew and we made them ourselves. It was incredibly frustrating: we had all this press coverage and we couldn't get our products into the stores. We worked a lot of late nights, and worked so hard that I've never wanted to sew again! And, of course, I didn't have any money to pay people, so they got paid in knickers.

Other labels started to produce very similar garments, and I felt that some of them had infringed what's known as my unregistered design rights. It was essential for the business that I defended those rights, and I was incredibly fortunate that my dad had worked with one of the world's leading copyright lawyers, who agreed to represent me. His was the kind of expertise that you can't normally buy – there was no way I could have afforded him if he hadn't been a family friend. He got paid in knickers too, to give to his daughters. He still works regularly with me on what I feel are continued infringements and, thanks to him, companies including La Perla, River Island and New Look have ceased producing designs that he successfully argued had infringed my rights.

At the end of my first year of trading, I was approached by people such as Marks & Spencer, Top Shop and Victoria's Secret to design a high-street collection for them. Although I was very flattered, I realised that if I created my own diffusion line, I wouldn't have to share the profits with them. So I created the Mimi Holliday brand within which pieces retail at £25–50, and did an exclusive deal with House of Fraser to stock it. I agreed to the exclusivity on the condition that they bought a certain number of units from me. Even though it sold very well for them, they couldn't sell enough stock to justify the large order and so the contract wasn't continued. That left us with a £500,000 hole in our revenues: it could easily have devastated the business, but we've built back up from there and last year our turnover was £800,000; next year I'm conservatively predicting it will be £1.4 million.

The business is in a very comfortable place: we have a small team of three with everything such as accountancy, warehousing and PR outsourced. Sales are tripling each season for Mimi Holliday, and doubling for Damaris. Orders are still coming to us rather than us going looking for them, so this is probably how we'll stay for a couple of years. In the long term, I have the option of bringing in finance, which might enable us to open our own shop, or to have concessions in department stores. The one thing I'm sure of is that I will start another business at some point. I can see that I will get bored, and I love the business side of things as much as the design side, so I will definitely be looking around for another venture.

What's the best advice you've ever had? I'm still very thankful that someone suggested approaching the Prince's Trust, but mostly I am grateful for the way I was raised. I was always told that if I wanted something enough, I would be capable of making it happen.

What do you wish you'd known from the start? I think my experience with the House of Fraser order has taught me the benefits of starting small. And it would have made a big difference if we could have found a reliable factory at the beginning. I now get my garments made in Shanghai and the quality is amazing.

What's the one thing you'd say to someone starting their first business? You've got to be completely and utterly obsessed with it. When it's your first business, you've got to live and breathe it. Which means you've got to love what you do.

8 Millionaire

I guess this is the bit you've been waiting for. How do you turn all that hard work into a fortune? If you have a successful company, then there are a number of ways you can seek to get cash out of it, but if your company is struggling, it may be that the most you can take from it is experience. And that's no bad thing.

Calling it a day

Most successful entrepreneurs have started several businesses by the time they launch the one that makes them a fortune. If you come to the conclusion that your business isn't the vehicle that will make you rich – and assuming that's your ultimate goal – then you have the option of calling it a day and starting your second business. It's positive decisions like this that lead to negative statistics about 50 per cent of new businesses 'failing'.

When you do it all over again, you will have so much experience under your belt of everything from managing relationships with suppliers to managing cashflow, that you will find you can make much faster progress the second time around. You will also have built up credibility with banks and investors, a factor that could make the difference with your next venture.

I see my ice-cream business as my degree in entrepreneurship. Instead of spending four years at university and ending up in debt, I spent five years learning about business from being in business, rather than from lectures and books. If your first business doesn't make it, this is how I suggest you view your experience: as a first-class education of the kind that money can't buy.

Your first business is a prestigious qualification that puts you in a great position to make a success of whatever you do next. The Americans have a much more enlightened attitude towards entrepreneurs – the 'rags to riches' story is part of the American dream – and there are even investors who would rather back you if you have a business failure on your CV! They believe that failure teaches you more than success: I'm not sure that's true, but I do think that it teaches you just as much as success. You should therefore always talk about your first business with pride, regardless of its eventual fate.

Of course, you don't have to wait for your business to hit the buffers before you call it a day. You may simply have had a better idea, or become bored, or be anticipating a change in the future that will damage your prospects. Whatever your reasons, there is no shame in calling time on a business that is no longer lighting your fire.

If your first business doesn't make it, I suggest you view your experience as a first-class education of the kind that money can't buy.

Running it for pleasure

Many people say that they love their company like one of the family and that they can't imagine life without it. They get a kick out of working with a great team, they know their products and services are appreciated, and it provides them with a decent income and a great quality of life. If that sounds like your business, who cares if you're a millionaire or not? Remember that Bob Dylan quote – 'A man is a success if he gets up in the morning and gets to bed at night, and in between he does what he wants to do.' I think it's absolutely true, and I wouldn't suggest to anyone that the only successful businesses are the ones with multi-million-pound valuations.

There are, however, a couple of pieces of advice I would like to give to business owners who choose this path. Firstly, keep doing your SWOT analyses every six months. When you're comfortable, it's surprisingly easy to become complacent, and this leaves you vulnerable to the competition. And secondly, never take your customers for granted. Make it your job to find out what they want, what they think of you and how you can hold on to them.

Selling up

In most industries, there is a standard way of valuing a company, and that is almost always a multiple of your profits. For example, Bannatyne Health Clubs paid nine times profit when we acquired a chain of 24 clubs in 2006 (for leasehold clubs the multiple was six times profit). So if I wanted to buy a freehold club that makes £1 million a year, the owner could expect me to pay £9 million for it. You can get a good idea of the multiple in your industry by looking at the comparable publicly listed companies in the *Financial Times*. However, the published figure is only a guide, and if the markets are keen on your sector, then your multiple will go up. If your sector is in decline, then it will fall.

As with every market, the key factor in setting the price is supply and demand. If there are lots of players looking to get a toehold in your sector (perhaps because of recently introduced tax reliefs), then you could find yourself at the centre of a bidding war. Similarly, if lots of companies in your industry are offered up for sale at the same time, then the prices will be kept more realistic.

When I sold my day-care nurseries, several companies tendered for the business, which had a profit of about £1 million a year at the time. We got several bids around the £7 million mark, which is what we were expecting, and then a stunning bid of £22 million came in from Alchemy Partners. The reason they paid so much was new government legislation that required all venture capital trusts to invest 70 per cent of their funds in qualifying industries, and at the time, day care was one of those industries. If they hadn't invested in these areas, their backers would not have been eligible for tax breaks that had encouraged them to put their money into Alchemy's trust in the first place. I was lucky. I had no idea about the new legislation. It's certainly worth finding out if there is something similar in your industry that could radically change the valuation of your company.

So how do you sell a company? One of the most effective ways is simply telling a few well-placed contacts that you think it's time to move on to the next challenge and that you would be open to offers. The chances are that you will be bought by another company already in your sector who will want to leverage your customer base and create economies of scale by merging the two companies. Your contacts within the industry can therefore act as very able selling agents. Alternatively, you can advertise the business for sale in local and trade magazines, or you can employ an agent who – like estate agents – will charge a percentage of the final price for handling the sale.

It's fairly standard for the founder and their management team to be bought as part of the deal. As much of the value of your company actually resides in your head, you can expect to be asked to sign a 'handcuff' deal that ties you to the company for a handover period, which can be anything up to five years. Although you will be paid some of the money when the deal is signed, the rest can be kept as a kind of 'good-behaviour bond' and will only be paid at the end of the handcuff period when agreed targets have been met.

It might be that your business is more valuable sold in parts. Perhaps your database is valuable to one company, your premises to another company, and your existing contracts to yet another. This can make you very attractive to buyers as they know they can make a profit by breaking up the company and selling the pieces on. But, of course, they shouldn't be the ones to make that money, you should. If you can bear to break the company up, this might be a way of maximising the price.

A word of warning before you sell: I have bumped into several friends who have sold businesses for millions and, at the time of the sale, looked forward to lazy days on the golf course or with their kids. A few months on and it's surprising how many will tell you that they regret selling. 'Life's a bit boring now. I really miss it.' That's why I know I will never sell my last business, whatever that happens to be. Until the day I die, there will be an office I can pop into, staff I can chat to and deals I can negotiate. If you enjoy business, I don't think a lazy retirement will be enough.

Once you've sold up, you can't turn round in six months' time and say, 'I've changed my mind. Give it back!'

Franchising

Some of the biggest names on the high street are franchise operations. Businesses as diverse as McDonald's, the Body Shop and Kall Kwik all grew through franchising, and if you have a replicable business, you could do the same.

In a nutshell, franchising works like this: you teach someone to do exactly what you have done and give them all the tools and support they need to do it; in exchange, they pay you an initial fee and then an annual payment thereafter, typically a percentage of their turnover. Depending on your business, the initial fee may be just a few hundred pounds for a house-cleaning business, up to around £500,000 for a prime McDonald's location.

The benefit to the franchisor – you – is that you can grow your business very quickly without needing to raise cash, as the franchisees meet their own start-up costs because each franchise is a separate company. Instead of you opening several outlets in succession, a team of franchisees can open them simultaneously.

Not all businesses are suitable for franchising, but if you think yours is, then you need to ask yourself why someone would pay to be your franchisee rather than just copy what you've done and keep all the profits for themselves. Although there are plenty of reasons why people choose to become franchisees rather than start from scratch, the value of your franchise operation will almost certainly be in your brand. So if you think that your business might be franchiseable, then you need to set about obtaining trademarks and shoring up your intellectual property rights.

The contracts between franchisers and franchisees are extraordinarily detailed and set out how a relationship will work over decades and what your responsibilities are to each other. It is not a job for amateurs and you will probably find the whole thing easier if you use a franchise consultant. You can find a reputable one through the British Franchise Association (www.thebfa.org). It's an area that attracts a few sharks, who only want to flog franchises to unsuspecting people who think they can make money rather than earn money, and some even charge the franchisor thousands of pounds, so really check out the credentials of the firms you deal with.

If everything goes well, you should be able to sell your existing business to a franchisee, and step back to oversee the franchise network while employing an MD to do the hard work for you!

Management buy-out

You might find, when you talk to your senior staff about your plans to sell up, that they tell you they don't want to work for a new boss. They have been working in the business for years and know it backwards, so it's only natural they'd resent a new boss coming in and changing things.

If your staff care about the company and your customers as much as you do, they might want to buy it from you themselves. As employees, they probably don't have the kind of cash you are hoping your business is worth, but there are a number of investors who will have the money.

Let's say your business is worth £1 million. Your management team goes to a private equity house that agrees to invest the money in exchange for, say, 70 per cent of the business. Your management team get the remaining 30 per cent. You get your £1 million and your team get to keep their jobs and run the business. The catch is that the investor will want two things from your management team: 70 per cent of the profits or dividends, and an exit strategy. Does your team intend to expand the company, acquire rivals, impose efficiencies or put up prices? They need to know how they will make the company more profitable so that the investor will be able to sell their shares at a profit in the future. Often MBOs, as they're called, are followed a couple of years later by a stock-market flotation when the management team get their hands on some of the value they've created.

Get yourself a Nigel

As I said at the beginning of this book, usually I spend about five hours a week in the office. Of course, my companies don't run themselves: my brilliant managing director Nigel Armstrong does.

Nigel's been with me for over ten years. He started as a financial controller and worked his way up. He loves the business as much as I do and he's worked with me long enough to know my attitude to most situations: from a club that's suffering from a poor manager to the chance to acquire several acres of land, Nigel knows what decision I would make and makes it himself.

Most of my time in the office is spent with Nigel, talking over the bigger deals and assessing future opportunities, but the day-to-day management is down to him. Sometimes all I have to do is sign the paperwork.

At Quality Care Homes, much of the operational activity was handled by my finance director Chris Rutter, and I consider myself lucky to have found both Chris and Nigel as it's not easy to run somebody else's company for them. The key is to make sure they are incentivised to do the job as well as you would do it. I structure Nigel's salary so that he gets a very healthy bonus if he meets the growth targets I set him and he also benefits from share options that will make him a millionaire one day.

As you build your business, you should look out for the Nigels and Chrises of this world, because finding that lieutenant who can take over gives you so many options. You get to keep a business you love, you get time to spend on other things, you don't get bored, and the best bit is, they grow the business and make you richer!

So if there's someone on your team who's showing promise, give them a bit more responsibility and get them to work closely with you for a while. Mould them to be the kind of manager you want them to be, and then tell them what you've got in mind for them. Get them to share your vision for the future and then watch them make it a reality.

Flotation

Depending on the size of your company, you have the option of floating on AIM, the Alternative Investment Market, or the main stock exchange if your company meets certain conditions. As with selling your company, investors will probably want you to remain with the company for a decent period after the flotation. To keep you motivated to make as much profit as you can for the shareholders, investors like to limit the number of shares a founder can sell. They want your wealth to be in the company, not in your bank account, and although you might be allowed to sell enough shares to make you comfortably well off, you will have to wait a few more years before you can sell the rest of your shares and leave the company.

I chose flotation for Quality Care Homes because it allowed me to a) keep control of the company, b) realise some of my capital, and c) raise funds from the stock market that allowed rapid expansion. I found the transition from answering only to myself to answering to a board of investors quite challenging, and the clashes between my entrepreneurial drive and the City's officious processes and procedures drove me nuts.

Changing from a privately to a publicly owned company is a huge upheaval, but it's also an amazing experience to see the company you started transformed by millions of pounds of investment. You have to accept that your corporate culture will change and you'll be answering to shareholders as well as your customers, but if you can ride that wave, then there is no better way to improve your company's, and your own, fortune.

You will need a broker to handle your flotation, and a list of suitable brokers is available from the stock exchange. All I did was call them up until I found a broker who dealt with my size of business and who I thought I could get along with. The process is a long one and from the initial phone call to receiving your cheque will probably take the best part of a year. First, the broker will get your business ready for the market, and that will probably mean imposing a chairman and a board of directors on you, all of whom will make you credible in the eyes of investors. They will all also expect a salary – sometimes £20,000–£30,000 a year just for attending a few board meetings! – and shares when the company floats. Your accounts will have to be audited by one of the big City firms of accountants (for a huge fee, of course) and a brochure telling investors about your business will need to be produced (for another fee). There will then be an endless tour of institutional investors like the pension funds who will want to understand your plans for growth and what they will mean for your share price.

At every stage, the fees for the accountants, the brokers, the non- executive directors and their expenses are enormous, in fact they will probably take your breath away, but not half as much as the day your broker phones to tell you, 'Congratulations, you are now officially a millionaire.'

● ● ● ● ● BANNATYNE'S BOOTCAMP ● ● ● ● ●

Getting what you want

1   Keep focused on the big picture and don't get distracted by anything that keeps you from your ultimate goals.

2   Make sure the people around you know what is expected of them and incentivise them to produce the results.

3   Actions speak louder than words: don't talk about it, do it. And when you have to talk, say as little as possible. The less people know about you, the harder you are to read and I think this has helped me gain a reputation for being a bit hard. I'm tough, sure, but mostly I just don't talk too much.

4   Work hard. The one thing that makes a difference in business, the single thing responsible for creating the most amount of wealth in the history of economics isn't luck, or contacts, or legislation, it is graft. And lots of it.

● ●

IIIIIIIIIIIIIIIIIIIIIIIIIIIIIIIIIIII **CASE STUDY** IIIIIIIIIIIIIIIIIIIIIIIIIIIIIIIII

Name: Ray Taylor **Age**: 49
Job: CEO, Co-incidence; co-founder, Entrepreneurs Unite
Qualifications: O levels, A levels, dropped out of university
www.entrepreneursunite.com

My dad was very independent in his thinking, had high Christian stan-dards and strict rules of conduct for his family. He also had a sense of honour, drive and determination that enabled him to build a success-ful career in insurance. He was a big influence on me, and when he was diagnosed with multiple sclerosis when I was ten, it gave me an enormous sense of urgency to live life to the full.

I had hearing problems when I was young and subsequently was never seen as particularly bright at school, and I always felt that I was behind my peers. My brother won a scholarship to a St Albans boys' public school, but I went to the only school in Hertfordshire that would have me! When I finished school with poor results, my dad suggested I do business studies at college, where I soon discovered that material things like cars helped to attract girls. So, starting with £50, I bought and sold anything I could until I had the money for a shiny second-hand TVR.

I didn't really see the point of college and only did enough to get me on to a management-training course with the Forward Trust, part of Midland Bank (now HSBC). The course gave me a series of two-month stints with different senior managers and directors of the company. The placements were meant to last for two years, but I only managed four months. Although I enjoyed working with the people, I quickly realised that progress depended on convincing others of my abilities. These 'others' were in a hierarchy that was largely based on years of service rather than competency. I also began to hate the snobbery and injustice created by hierarchical structures: I knew I needed to work 'with' rather than 'for' people.

I felt the only answer was to start my own business. With no idea what it should be, I started to talk to anyone who was apparently successful. My next-door neighbour had a string of nice cars in his drive, and when he told me that he ran a successful printing company, I decided I would become a printer too. In just three months, with no training or proper planning, I had sold my car, bought a printing press with the money, persuaded an old schoolfriend to join me, and had started operating out of a building between two turkey sheds on a nearby farm.

However, I very quickly realised that value was generated out of the content *on* the paper, not the means by which it was printed. I was in the wrong business: I wanted to start producing the content.

The father of a college friend owned a local coach company that took old ladies on regular holidays. I heard he was inviting agencies to pitch for an advertising campaign that he had a £15,000 budget for. I persuaded him to let me pitch for the contract, and without knowing anything about pitching or advertising, I interviewed him so that I could understand his ambitions for the company, and how he made his money. This allowed me to define his business objectives. I then did the same with the old ladies that went on his trips, and tried to understand their circumstances, their likes and dislikes. By matching up the two I was able to devise my own strategy. I pretty well tore up the original brief and asked a freelance designer to help me out with some visuals. We won the business with an increased price tag of £18,000.

Over the next few years I applied the same formula, ignoring the standard practices of the marketing industry, and learning from every experience. I hired people based on their attitude, skill and passion rather than their experience, and in just ten years I had a team of 250 people with an average age of 26, and ran the UK's largest independent branding agency.

With no formal training, I achieved success by keeping my feet firmly on the ground and by simply applying common sense to everything we did. We also worked incredibly hard, and as a consequence we worked at board level with some of the brightest people in the UK at companies like Marks & Spencer and Barclays and helped them develop some of the world's most powerful brands. I also discovered something remarkable: that when I was passionate about a project, the shyness I usually experienced disappeared. Passion was the key to overcoming obstacles and to creating success. The company continued to grow, both nationally and internationally, and was eventually sold in 2000.

For the first time in my life I had what the moneymen call 'liquidity', but those I went to for financial advice talked about money as if it had a virtue in its own right, which I found profoundly depressing. The very success I had been conditioned to believe was the point of all that work was depressingly empty. I realised the value of money to me was as a unit of exchange that could be used to make things happen.

I calculated that, provided I controlled my greed, I had enough money to keep the fridge full for the rest of my life, which is a wonderful position to be in. I began to admire the people who had reached this conclusion without first having to 'win' in a materialistic way. I also began to reflect on how I had become successful, and I realised that when my passion and drive to make things happen had overcome my shyness, I had been able to persuade people of my opinion. This passion had been a direct consequence of seeking the truth in something, and coming to a deep understanding of the subject matter in hand.

It struck me that this deep understanding, this dedication, seemed to prompt what outsiders might have perceived as 'coincidences', i.e. where the world appeared to conspire to support judgements and activities I was involved with. But I knew that these coincidences were the consequence of my dedication. I therefore decided to follow the concept of coincidence and see where it took me. I started a small investment company, which I called Co-incidence, that backs people and adventures that can bring about positive change.

As part of this journey I had the opportunity to share an idea with Richard Branson, who, in turn, invited me to go to South Africa with his charity, Virgin Unite, and some other entrepreneurs. During the trip, the entrepreneurs naturally started to plot and scheme ways to help change some of the clear injustices of the area. In fact, the energy that emerged was immense. I had a strong sense that it sparked a light in many of us to try to achieve things that could really make a difference.

By 'coincidence' I then met Duncan Bannatyne at a conference. We talked about my experiences in South Africa, and he recounted his similar experiences in Romania and Malawi where he'd built orphanages and funded a schooling programme. The idea came to me of setting up a club that brought successful entrepreneurs together to use their skills, networks, kudos and cash to bring about change in impoverished areas. That club is called Entrepreneurs Unite, and following the principles of coincidence, I decided to drive it.

People say to me now that I must have been very smart to get where I am, but the truth is that life isn't like that. You look at your universe of opportunities, you have an idea, you put your head down and run off at top speed in one direction, then in six months' time you look up and see what's changed. Your universe of opportunities will be different, so you assess the best route and change direction if necessary. The path we all take is a bit of a zigzag. Then someone looks at where you are now, draws a straight line back to where you started and thinks you must be a genius! But all any of us do is assess the opportunities around us and respond to them. That's what I tell people who want to be in business: you can't know everything at the start. I bet Bill

Gates wasn't thinking about the Windows operating system when he was playing around with computers in his garage.

What's the best advice you've ever had? This is something I figured out for myself: if you create demand then capital will follow. If you have a new business that's untried and you seek investment, you'll have to give away a lot of equity. But if you can demonstrate demand, then you reduce the risk and investors will take a lower percentage.

What do you wish you'd known from the start? Nothing really. That's not to say that I didn't make mistakes, but falling over occasionally is all part of being in business. Success is a very poor teacher, and I believe mistakes are valuable. However, the ability to listen more when I was younger might have helped. I was so dogmatic and stubborn that no one could sway me, and then a year later I'd think that maybe I shouldn't have done something that someone had advised me against!

What's the one thing you'd say to someone starting their first business? Don't take any short cuts, do everything to the best of your ability, create demand and worry about capital later. It's really important to get the balance right between having a good idea and then going for it. Don't be swayed: you have to follow something with passion and determination for at least six months before you can assess how well it's going.

List of resources

There is so much help out there for budding entrepreneurs that I'm not going to attempt to compile a complete directory of resources as it's probably a book in itself. The organisations on my list are just your starting points for further investigation, and a quick Google search will throw up more options than you could ever need.

Business Link
www.businesslink.gov.uk
This is the agency tasked with enabling new businesses to find their feet. Get practical advice on everything from grants to health and safety, and make use of their great helplines.

Companies House
www.companieshouse.gov.uk
Find information on incorporating your business and becoming a limited company, and find out who the directors of your rival companies are.

Department for Business, Enterprise and Regulatory Reform

www.berr.gov.uk

Find information on the latest government incentives and schemes for fostering enterprise. The Small Business Unit has the most useful information at www.berr.gov.uk/bbf/enterprise-smes/index.html.

Financial Services Authority

www.fsa.gov.uk

Find out about banks and banking regulations, and check out if the lender you're dealing with meets their criteria and standards.

Health and Safety Executive

www.hse.gov.uk

Find out about your responsibilities to staff, clients and customers.

HM Revenue & Customs

www.hmrc.gov.uk

Find information about registering for VAT, self-employment and the tax implications of becoming an employer. There is also a neat overview of starting a business at www.hmrc.gov.uk/startingup/indcx.htm.

Intellectual Property Office

www.ipo.gov.uk

Find information about protecting your ideas through trademarks and patents.

London Stock Exchange

www.londonstockexchange.com

Find information on plcs, and investigate your flotation options.

Money Saving Expert

www.moneysavingexpert.com

Whatever you're spending money on, the chances are you could be getting everything that little bit cheaper. Keeping your costs down in the early days can make a big difference, and I think there is some really useful information on Martin Lewis's site that could help any new business save money.

Money Supermarket

www.moneysupermarket.com

Use their search tools to find the cheapest financial deals out there, from loans to insurance. There are many similar sites, so it might be worth trying a few of them.

Pensions

www.pensionsregulator.gov.uk

www.thepensionservice.gov.uk

Use these two sites to check out your obligations regarding your staff's pension entitlements.

Index